A
BRIEF HISTORY
OF THE
BHOPAL PRINCIPALITY
IN
CENTRAL INDIA

A BRIEF HISTORY OF THE BHOPAL PRINCIPALITY IN CENTRAL INDIA

WILLIAM HOUGH

GYAN

Published by

Gyan Publishing House
5, Ansari Road
Daryaganj, New Delhi-110002
Phone: 011-47034999, 9811692060
E-mail: books@gyanbooks.com

Distribution Network
gyanbooks.com
India, USA, Canada, UK, Australia

ISBN: 978-93-6780-175-8 (HB)

First Published, 1845

2nd Impression 2024

Printed at: Gyan Press, Delhi.

A BRIEF HISTORY OF THE BHOPAL PRINCIPALITY IN CENTRAL INDIA

Author: WILLIAM HOUGH

A
BRIEF HISTORY
OF THE
BHOPAL PRINCIPALITY
IN
CENTRAL INDIA.

FROM THE PERIOD OF
ITS
FOUNDATION,
ABOUT ONE HUNDRED AND FIFTY YEARS AGO,
TO THE
PRESENT TIME.

BY
WILLIAM HOUGH, MAJOR,
BENGAL ESTABLISHMENT.

CALCUTTA:
PRINTED AT THE BAPTIST MI
CIRCULAR ROAD.

1845.

INTRODUCTION.

The exact period when Dost Mahomed founded the Bhopal principality is not stated in any printed work. He was born in the year 1657, and came, when young, to Delhi, it may be supposed, about the year 1680. It is, therefore, probable that the Bhopal principality was founded about 150 years ago; at a period when many of the existing principal Native powers were but small states.

In the year 1778, when the Bombay and Supreme Government had determined to place Ragoba *(Ragonath Rao)* on the throne of Poonah, as Peshwah,—a measure distasteful to the principal party at that Court, and to the Mahrattahs; the latter confederated against the Bombay Government, and assembled, as acknowleged by themselves, 60,000 horse. The Bombay Government sent a force consisting of 4,000 men (of whom there were 700

Europeans) to accompany Ragonauth Rao, who had a force of 20,000 men, to Poonah. The Bombay force was surrounded in the *Bhore Ghat* and on the 15th of January, 1779, was compelled to sign the memorable treaty of *Wurgaum*. General *Goddard* was then on his march to assist the Bombay Government, but was at a considerable distance It is stated in the *Annual Register* for 1782 (1) that —" they (the Bombay Committee) informed *Sindia* they had brought a blank paper signed and sealed by the committee and principal military officers, which the Mahrattah chiefs were to fill up as they pleased. *Sindia,* with moderation and wisdom, advised the Mahrattah council not to take any unreasonable advantage of their own power, and of the distress and necessity of the *English:* for, he said, 'our making large demands would only sow resentment in their hearts, and we had better demand only what is necessary. Let *Ragonauth Rao,* be with us, and the treaty between us and the English will be adhered to.' " This Sindia was *Madhajee* Sindiah, the uncle of *Dowlut Rao* Sindiah mentioned in this work.

(1) Page 15 to 22 History. I have no where else found this information.

BHOPAL PRINCIPALITY.

THE

PRINCIPALITY OF BHOPAL

THE History of the Bhopal Principality is one of the most interesting of the Native States in India (1). The Mahomedan and Hindoo authorities, though they agree as to the principal facts in the life of Dost Mahomed Khan, the founder of the Bhopal family, are at variance with regard to several of the details connected with his establishment of independent power. This chief came, when young, from Affghanistan to Delhi, where he entered the service of a nobleman (2), of the same Affghan tribe, (3) to which he himself belonged. Dost Mahomed appears shortly after his arrival to have quitted the service of his countryman, and entered that of the emperor Aurungzeb. He was one of the

(1) Sir John Malcolm in his "Central India," vol I pp 349 to 425, 3rd edition, 1832, has given a very interesting account of the Nuwabs of Bhopal, from which, and from the works of Captain James Grant Duff, and H. T. Prinsep, Esq., I have chiefly taken my information

(2) Jelal Khan.

(3) The Mirajee Kheil.

party detached into Malwa, where he succeeded in bringing himself to the notice of the governor of the province by his gallantry, and was in consequence rewarded by a nomination to the superintendence of the district of Bersiah (4), the revenues of which are stated to have been then greatly reduced by the unceasing depredations of freebooters.

The progress of Dost Mahomed subsequent to this period was very rapid. He first became possessed of Juddeespoor, which was changed into the Mahomedan name of Islamnuggur, and became the capital of Dost Mahomed He next obtained possession of Bhopal, where he settled with his family and their adherents, whom he had invited from Affghanistan Dost Mahomed after this captured Cheynpoor Barree and Gunnour, when he increased his army, and adopted measures to enable him to preserve the territories he had obtained. He built a citadel within the limits of the town of Bhopal, which he named Futtygurh; having connected this with the town and enclosed the latter by a wall, gave to the whole a security which was indispensable to the object he had in view, viz. to increase the population and prosperity of his capital.

About three years before the death of Dost Mahomed Khan, Nizam-ul-Moolk, who was

(4) A town in the Mahrattah territories, in the province of Malwa, 30 miles from Bhopal, lat 23° 42′ N. long. 77° 32′ E.

proceeding towards the Dekhan from Malwa, (of which province he had been for a short time governor), sought the friendship of the Affghan chief against the Court of Delhi, which treatened him with an attack Dost Mahomed, from political motives, not only declined the Nizam's alliance, but acceded to the requisition of his enemies, by aiding them with a force under his brother (Meer Mahomed Khan), who was slain in an action that ensued, in which the Nizam obtained the victory. The Affghan chief, alarmed at having incurred the resentment of so powerful a prince, offered his, then, only son (Yar Mahomed Khan) as an hostage for his future good conduct. The Nizam satisfied with this pledge, left him in tranquil possession of the countries he had subdued, and formed into a principality

Dost Mahomed died at the age of 66 (5). He assumed the title of nuwab after the death of Aurungzeb, and it was amid the disturbances of that period that he formed the Principality of Bhopal. Whatever might have been his defects, there can be no doubts of his talents He was deemed, even in a tribe where valour is a common quality, a man of remarkable courage. His life was for more than 30 years

(5) As Aurungzeb died on 21st February 1707, the Bhopal Principality must have been formed about 40 years ago, as Dost Mahomed came to Hindostan some years before the emperor's death

one scene of warfare; he had received in action above 30 wounds; and his memory as a soldier is still fondly cherished by the family of which he was the founder.

1723 On the death of Dost Mahomed Khan, the ministers at the Court of Bhopal elevated Sultan Mahomed Khan to the musnud, or throne, to the prejudice of his elder brother, Yar Mahomed Khan, who had been carried into the Dekhan as an hostage by Nizam-ul-Moolk The pretext for this act was the absence of Yar Mahomed Khan; but the real motive was a desire to conduct the affairs of the state during a long minority. Sultan Mahomed Khan was a child of 7 or 8 years of age, while his absent brother was a youth of 18 or 20. The attempt, however, was not successful. The cause of Yar Mahomed was espoused by Nizam-ul-Moolk, and he was sent to Bhopal with the title of nuwab, escorted by a thousand horse. He also received from Nizam-ul-Moolk the high insignia of the Maha Muratib, or the dignity of the Fish, one of the first honors of the Moghul empire. This is still assumed as a hereditary honor by the nuwabs of Bhopal No opposition was made to his return; but though Sultan Mahomed Khan was compelled by the puthan chiefs to abdicate, they would not instal Yar Mahomed as Prince, being an illegitimate son; on the pretext that the usages of his tribe prohibited his inheriting the name of Prince; but, that there was no objection to his exercising all the royal functions (6) The arrangements which took place on this occasion explain the origin of feelings which still exist, and give to the puthan colony at Bhopal a very peculiar constitution When Dost Mahomed had, after his first successes, invited his brethren and kinsmen to join him, they were accompanied by his elder brother, Akil Mahomed Khan, who being at the head of a party attached to the usages of their country, with a view to keep these unchanged, established certain rules for the regulation of all their personal and family affairs, which were deemed as imperative upon their chiefs and princes as upon the most obscure individuals of the tribe. Akil Mahomed Khan was first in rank among these Affghans, and his excellent character merited the distinction which his birth and their good opinion assigned him. This respectable nobleman was dewan, or prime minister. On his death (7),

(6) Major Henley states, in his notes upon the Bhopal family, that Yar Mahomed's succession to power arose from motives of policy, rather than from any precise rule on the subject Akil Mahomed (the elder brother of Dost Mahomed) saw the necessity of complying as much as possible with the wishes of the Nizam, but it was settled that on Sultan Mahomed's entering the Durbar, Yar Mahomed should from courtesy rise to receive him, and moving aside from the musnud, allow him to sit on the right

(7) Akil Mahomed Khan was murdered at the hoolee He was great-grand-father to Kurreem Khan, who was dewan in 1832

the office was conferred on Byjeeram, a Hindoo, to whom Islamnuggur owes its principal improvements : he built a palace, and augmented its strength by diverting the course of the Parwah, so as to make that river a ditch to its fortifications.

1737. There are few particulars given of Yar Mahomed's life. He was succeeded by his eldest son (8), Feyz Mahomed Khan, who was then 11 years of age. The pretensions of his uncle, Sultan Mahomed Khan, were again brought forward by a strong party of Affghan lords. Feyz Mahomed, however, had been placed on the throne, and the army, amounting to 5000 men, remained firm to his interests. Supported by them, he made every preparation to resist the attack with which he was threatened The Mahjee Sahibah, or lady mother (as the widow of Yar Mahomed was called), despatched a man of religious character, named Shah Allum, with a body of Rohillahs (puthans), to seize Sultan Mahomed The latter at first concealed himself, but in an affray which followed, Shah Allum was killed, and his party repulsed. On this intelligence reaching Islamnuggur, Byjeeram, with the young nuwab and his followers, immediately advanced towards Bhopal ; and Sultan

(8) Yar Mahomed had four sons, Feyz Mahomed Khan, Hiyat Mahomed Khan, Yasseen Mahomed Khan, and Seid Mahomed Khan

Mahomed with his Affghans marched to receive them. Imitating the usage of the Hindoo saints and warriors, they dyed their garments with yellow (9), the hymeneal colour, which indicated, that they went to battle as to a bridal feast, and were determined to die, or to live exulting conquerors.

Byjeeram, whose numbers were superior, saw with pleasure his enemies quit the protection they had in the walls of Bhopal. He drew up in line of battle; but his troops, who were chiefly Hindoos, would probably have been broken by the furious charge of the Affghans, had not these, when exhausted by their first success, been attacked, and in their turn routed by the desperate Rohillahs of Shah Allum, who continued faithful to the cause of Feyz Mahomed, and were eager to revenge the death of their late commander. The assailants were in their turn, defeated; their chief, Sultan Mahomed, fled to Seronj, whence he went to the hill fort of Rathgurh, into which he was admitted by the governor. Here, he was immediately besieged by Byjeeram; but the Mahjee Sahibah, or lady mother, seeing the evil of these family dissensions, interposed her authority, through the influence of which Rath-

(9) A dye made from the flower called Kuswur in Hindoostanee. Using it on the day of battle, is among the Hindoos deemed a sacred pledge to die or conquer. Volunteers are often invited to assume the yellow dress, which implies desperation in any undertaking

gurh, with its dependencies were bestowed, in free grant, to Sultan Mahomed and his descendants; but they were precluded, by the same agreement, from all future pretensions to the sovereignty, or any interference with the management of the Bhopal territory.

The termination of these disputes was probably accelerated by a sense of common danger. The Peshwah, Bajerow, while returning from Dehli, encamped on the plains between Lahore and Ashta and required, in the name of the emperor, whom he represented as soobahdar, or governor of Malwa, a restitution of all the lands which the Bhopal puthans had usurped. Resistance appeared unavailing, and the minister Byjeeram, negotiated a treaty by which the Bhopal government made a sacrifice of half its territories to save the remainder. By this engagement, it lost the whole of its possession in Malwa, except a few towns; what remained, which was chiefly in Gondwarra, was confirmed to the family by the treaty with the Peshwah.

Soon after the departure of the Mahrattahs, the discontent of the garrison which occupied the hill fort of Raiseen (10) gave Byjeeram an opportunity of making himself master of that place, which has ever since belonged to

(10) A town in the province of Malwa, the capital of a district of the same name, 126 miles east from Oujein, lat. 23° 19′ N. long. 77° 47′ E

the principality (11). The possession of it was afterwards confirmed by a sunnud from Delhi, which, as well as the title of "*Futteh Jung*," given at the same time, was paid for by the nuwab.

Byjeeram, the minister of Feyz Mahomed, was a man of talents, and the country of Bhopal attained a state of considerable prosperity under his management. He conciliated the Gonds (12), who are the aboriginal inhabitants of the southern portion of the Bhopal territory.

On Byjeeram's death he was succeeded by his son Gassyram, who had only been in office a twelve month, when he was destroyed by two puthan noblemen. Gassyram is said by the Affghan biographers to have conferred all offices on his Hindoo favorites, and even to have cut off the noses of butchers who attempted to kill oxen or buffaloes; and this account is confirmed by some respectable Hindoo writers.

(11) It was taken in 1798, but recaptured by Vizier Mahomed.

(12) This numerous class of Hindoos denominated Gonds, from their inhabiting Gondwarra, once held a high rank among the natives of this part of India, but they have been successively reduced by the Mahomedans and Mahrattahs, to a very low state. This tribe, who inhabit both banks of the Nerbudda, from near its source to as far west as Ongkar Mundatta, are spread over the greatest part of the Nagpoor territories They have a language and usages distinct from other classes of Hindoos.

On the death of Gassyram, a puthan named Ghyrut Khan succeeded to the office of dewan, which he held for six years, whenhe was poisoned by a courtesan. His successor was raja Keisoree, of the Kayastha tribe (13), who had been a writer with Byjeeram: he was a man of talent, and the country prospered for 14 years under his superindence; but he chiefly owes his celebrity to the circumstance of his massacre

Feyz Mahomed Khan, who had embraced a life of austerity and devotion, had still a haram filled with ladies: amongst them there was one known by the title of Begum, or princess, a native of Delhi Owing to some intrigue being suspected. between the son of the minister (Keisoree) and the daughter of Ashruff Khan, some puthan noblemen planned the minister's destruction. Both he and his son were murdered Keisoree's widow, on hearing this, destroyed herself and the females of the family, by blowing up her house with gunpowder The explosion caused by this event gave the first information to Feyz Mahomed of the fate of his minister, whose death he is said to have deplored. Yessein Khan, the nuwab's brother immediately assumed the functions of minister of the state. Nuwab Feyz Mahomed Khan, who had, nominally, governed Bhopal for 38 years, did

(13) All writers and accountants.

not long survive this event : he died of a dropsy, brought on by his sedentary habits, in the 48th or 49th year of his age. This prince was throughout his life a religious recluse, of very weak intellect, and of an enormous stature, being nearly seven feet high, and his hands, when he was standing, reached below his knees. He never but once went beyond the precincts of his palace Ghyrut Khan, when minister, carried him to Bhilsa, which had been for some time besieged, and it happened to fall soon after his arrival. The belief, which the ignorant Affghans entertained of the holy character of their chief was confirmed by this occurrence, and his memory is revered as that of a saint. Feyz Mahomed had no issue His brother Yessein Mahomed Khan was at the head of the government during the few days he survived him. At his death, Hiyat Mahomed Khan was proclaimed nuwab ; but he was also, from disposition and habits, a religious recluse, and the actual exercise of power continued with the person who held the office of minister.

1775. The whole revenue of Bhopal at this time amounted to about 20 lakhs of rupees, of which a portion of five lakhs value in land was set aside for the support of the nuwab. With this the minister had no concern ; it was managed in an office separate from those of the government, and the amount collected was appropriated according to the pleasure of the prince; but, beyond this, he and his personal attendants were considered to have no further claim on the public treasury, or any connexion whatever with state affairs. The history of Bhopal, while this system continued, consists in the proceedings of the dewans, or ministers.

Hiyat Mahomed Khan, when installed nuwab, had no children by his wife, but he had adopted four chelahs (14), or family dependants, who were considered almost as relations. The eldest of these, Fowlad Khan, was the son of a Gond. The second, Jumshere Khan, was the son of a Gossein; and the third and fourth, Chutta Khan and Islam Khan, were the sons of a brahmin. The merit of having withdrawn these children from their errors, to the true faith, no doubt, constituted, in the mind of a pious Mahomedan prince, another tie to strengthen that of adoption. Fowlad Khan, the eldest of the chelahs, was the first who possessed the power of minister.

1778. It was during his administration that the army under General *Goddard* passed through the territories of Bhopal. The inhabitants of the country are justly proud of the part their prince took upon this occasion; and with reason, for it was bold and decided

(14) Chelah means, literally, an adopted dependant; it neither applies to a slave, nor an adopted child, but to a person who is admitted to the claims of a dependant relation.

in a degree beyond what their condition warranted. Every aid required was freely given by this state; and, from the certificates still preserved by some of the heads of villages, it would seem that all ranks behaved in the most friendly manner to a body of men, who prized such conduct the more from having in other parts of their route, met with nothing but hostility. That the remaining part of the march of the Bengal force, after it passed the Nerbuddah, was unobstructed, may in some degree be ascribed to the conduct pursued by the puthans of Bhopal, whose behaviour on this memorable occasion, established a claim upon the British Government, which merited all the notice it has since received. In an official abstract made from the correspondence of General *Goddard* (15), it is stated that every effort was made to render the nuwab of Bhopal hostile to the English, but in vain; he remained true to his first promise of friendship, though many of his fields and villages were, in consequence, plundered by the Mahrattahs.

In addition to the testimony of Major General, Sir John *Malcolm*, may be given the account of another officer, who had ample

(15) Sir John Malcolm says, "I obtained this abstract of the proceedings of the Bengal detachment at Bombay. There are no records of the progress of this corps in the political office at Calcutta."

means of learning the nature of the friendship of the nuwab of Bhopal. Captain James Grant *Duff*, of the Bombay Army, in his History of the Mahrattahs (16) states, that "Colonel *Leslie* having died of a fever on the 3rd of October 1778, Colonel *Goddard* immediately assumed the command of the troops, and in a few days afterwards, commenced his march from Rajegurh (17), in Bundelkund, towards the Nerbuddah. His route lay by Mooltan, Kheinlassa, Beilsah, Bhopal and Hoossingabad ; at the last mentioned place he forded the Nerbuddah on the 2nd of December. Before Colonel *Goddard* had quitted the Bundelkund territory, Ballajee Punt, the Mahrattah officer stationed at Sagur, by whose machinations *Leslie's* progress was at first arrested, after many professions of friendship, made a perfidious attack on the baggage of the army, in which he was completely foiled. The conduct of the *Nuwab* of Bhopal was precisely the reverse of that of the Mahrattah officer; *he* treated the English with the greatest confidence and hospitality, furnished them with every supply and every possible assistance, at the risk of incurring future enmity from the Mahrattahs, without the support of his new

(16) Vol II. p. 384. A. D 1826. Formerly political Resident at Satara.

(17) A town on the west side of the river Cane, 18 miles south-east from Chatterpoor, in Bundelkund

friends. This generous behaviour, on the part of the Nuwab, was never forgotten; and it laid the foundation of a friendship, which, in modern times, has been laudably extended to his descendants by the British Government. After Colonel *Goddard* had crossed the Nerbuddah, he halted on the south bank of the river, to await some communications from Moodajee Bhonslay, particularly connected with his future operations."

There is a third testimony regarding the above transaction from the pen of H. T. Prinsep, Esq. (18), who had deeply studied the political affairs of India, and who, from his official position, had full knowledge of his subject. He says, alluding to the principality of Bhopal: "On a former occasion, when General *Goddard* was sent by Warren Hastings with an expedition from Hindoostan, in execution of his sagacious plan of alarming the Mahrattah powers, then confederated against us, into the acceptance of his own terms, by penetrating through the very heart of their possessions, the existence of this (*Bhopal*) independent principality was one of the principal encouragements to make the attempt.

(18) Narrative of the Political and Military Operations of British India under the administration of the Marquis of Hastings, 1813 to 1818—Quarto Edition, 1820, p. 39. Mr Prinsep was Persian Secretary to the Governor General, afterwards Secretary to the Government of India; and lastly a member of the Supreme Council of the Government of India.

The family are still in possession of the strongest testimonials from General *Goddard* of the important services rendered him by the reigning Nuwab (*Hyat Mahomed Khan*) (19); indeed, the ultimate success of the enterprise, and the final accomplishment of that officer's wonderful march across an enemy's country all the way to Surat, were mainly to be attributed to his having found this principality in a state of independence, and hostility to the Mahrattahs, midway on his line of march." Thus there are three well known authorities in proof of the friendly aid given by Bhopal, at a time when a British force was marching across India to the assistance of the Bombay Government, at a most critical period of the affairs of the East India Company. This assistance was afforded by a state which had nothing, apparently, to gain by such a generous act · while it is clear that it risked its very independence as a state, the moment the British force marched from the southern bank of the Nerbuddah. The result proved the danger it was exposed to, for Sir John *Malcolm* states that "many of his (the nuwab's) fields and villages were, in consequence of his fidelity to his engagement, plundered by the Mahrattahs." What other state, or power, has ever acted in a similar manner towards the British Government? The records of history are silent on the

(19) Grandfather of the present Begum mother of Bhopal.

subject: no parallel can be produced. Bhopal was not, at this time, in alliance with the British Government; nor under stipulation to assist the Army of General Goddard, it was, therefore, a generous, disinterested act, to which a parallel cannot be found in the history of British India *

Soon after the above events, a family quarrel occurred, in which Jowlad Khan was slain, in an attempt to capture the old fort of Bhopal, then the residence of the widow of Yar Mahomed Khan; who, from disgust at his resolute and tyrannical acts, had for some time resolved to subvert his authority, and to raise to power Chutta Khan, who she had taken care should be well instructed, that he might be competent to the duties of the high station. The history of this extraordinary princess, who lived to the advanced age of 80, and who for more than half a century greatly influenced, if she did not control, the councils of Bhopal, is very extraordinary. Her name was Mumullah; she came from Upper Hindoostan. Though never publicly married (20) to the Nuwab, Yar Mahomed, she became the principal lady of his family. She had herself

* It is to be hoped that the records of the above expedition may be requested to be sent to Calcutta, as they are much required to illustrate some important operations of the Bengal Army

(20) The *Nikah* was performed on her union with the Nuwab. This engagement, though inferior to marriage, is still respectable. It is common where the condition of the parties is too unequal to admit of one more legitimate.

no children, but all those of Yar Mahomed she considered as her own, and the title of Mahjee Sahibah, or Lady Mother, which was given her by them and all others, proves the respect in which she was held. From the account given of her conduct, under the most trying circumstances, it seems difficult to pronounce, whether she was most remarkable for the humanity of her disposition, or the excellence of her judgment. She was beloved and respected by all. Her memory is still cherished by the natives, both Hindoo and Mahomedan, of Bhopal, and it is consoling to observe, in the example of her life, that, even amid scenes of violence and crime, goodness and virtue, when combined with spirit and sense, maintain that superiority, which belongs alone to the higher qualities of human nature; and which, without these, can be permanently conferred by neither title nor station.

This virtuous woman had every reason to congratulate herself on her choice of Chutta Khan, who proved throughout his life, the friend of the poor, and the promoter of order and tranquillity; but, the determined resolution with which he pursued these objects, brought him into violent collision with several of the principal nobles of the state, some of whom were his enemies from the first, being indignant at the elevation of one whom they deemed so much their inferior. Two brothers,

Kumal Mahomed and Sheriff Mahomed, who were nearly related to the Nuwab, on the failure of a plot to possess themselves of Gunnour, retired with about 700 followers towards Sahore. Chutta Khan pursued them, and, in an engagement which took place, Sheriff Mahomed was slain. Kumal Mahomed effected his escape, though wounded, with the son of his brother. The latter, Vizier Mahomed, then a youth, lived to preserve his country; and to become the founder of the present family of Bhopal

Among the conspiracies formed against the power of Chutta Khan, one of the most remarkable was that of Nijabut Mahomed Khan, a turbulent Puthan chief, the son of Yassein Mahomed khan, whose object was to murder the Nuwab and ministers. This tragedy was to be acted on the last day of the Ramazan, when all the Affghans of the Nuwab's family were assembled at the house of the Mahjee, or Lady Mother, to pay their respects to that princess. The alarm of treason was given by a domestic, and the fierce chief, finding he was discovered, flew at the Nuwab, but was overpowered and slain, not without a great struggle, as he is represented to have been a man of immense strength and desperate courage. Three of the principal conspirators were killed at the same time; but not before they had cut down Rajah Bholanath, one of the principal Hindoo officers of the Government.

The above events, and others of a similar character, greatly irritated the mind of Chutta Khan, and urged him to very severe, if not oppressive, measures. This change of conduct is generally attributed to the death of the princess, by whom he had been raised to the high station of minister. He had certainly acted with great prudence and moderation while she lived, from respect to her advice, and confidence in her support; but when left alone, he saw his safety in another course. Enraged by the frequent conspiracies of the nobles against his power, he put to death some and expelled others. He removed this class from all offices of trust, which were filled exclusively by persons on whose attachment he could rely. He established such a police within the walls of Bhopal, as completely suppressed the sanguinary affrays, to which some Puthans are so prone, and their turbulent spirit was for the moment subdued. By these means, Chutta Khan not only maintained internal quiet, but promoted, beyond all who had gone before him, the prosperity of the town, and country of Bhopal. His next object was to remain at peace with his neighbours, but particularly with Madhojee Sindiah, and Ahalya Baee, who were, at this time, the chief rulers in central India. His principles of moderation were sometimes carried to an extent that astonished many. Of this, the following instance may be given A few years before his death, the Pindary leader, Hera Baee, plundered and burned some villages of Bhopal. Chutta Khan sent troops in pursuit of the depredators; and they returned with 400 naked prisoners, who had been stripped of their horses and clothes. When these people expected to be put to death, they were surprised to hear Chutta Khan direct that they should be released, and that each man should have a turban and a rupee to carry him back to his home. "Take this," he exclaimed, "but recollect you shall have other treatment if you come again into my country." When those around him looked surprised, he said, these poor creatures are, of themselves, no objects of vengeance; their leaders, from their connexion with the Mahrattah chiefs, are above my power; why outrage by useless violence those whose employers we cannot punish? They will now feel obliged by my humanity to their followers, who were in my power; and it will be an additional motive to make them refrain from attacking us." This occurrence and Chutta Khan's speech were stated by Khealee Ram, then a writer in his office, who witnessed and heard what he narrates, nor was Chutta Khan mistaken: during his life there were no more inroads made by these freebooters on the territories of Bhopal.

Chutta Khan was not above 40 years of age

when he died. Though he had been brought up a Mahomedan, he appears to have continued as much a Hindoo in his disposition, as he was in his appearance. He was of a moderate stature, slight make, temperate in his language, and smooth in his manners; he combined art with resolution, and was, in short, in every thing, the opposite of that tribe* to which he belonged by adoption.

On the death of Chutta Khan, efforts were made by several persons to obtain possession of his wealth. Nawaub, a Puthan officer, who had long been in his service, tried to make himself master both of his treasure and the Government; but after several acts of great violence, he was forced to leave Bhopal, carrying with him property to the supposed amount of six lakhs of rupees. He left the unprotected family of his late master to the oppression of their enemies The widow, after being plundered of every thing, was glad to escape alive. She was, in 1832, at Seronj, dependent for daily food on the Nuwab, Ameer Khan. Her only son, Ameer Mahomed, said to be a worthless character, was at the above time, one of the poorest followers of Guffoor Khan at Indore. Such has been the fate of the family of a man, who, by his management, raised Bhopal to the highest state of prosperity. But these reverses of fortune are too common in India to excite attention, much less commiseration.

1798. Himmut Row, a native of Upper Hindoostan, who had been during almost the whole of Chutta Khan's administration at the head of the revenue department, now received the title of Rajah, and was created Dewan, or Minister; but during the twelve months he held this office, he had hardly any power. Every thing was done by the Beebee (so Hiyat Mahomed Khan's favorite lady was called), and a eunuch of the name of Gul Khojah, in whom she confided; and among other ruinous expedients to which these persons had recourse to avert the dangers that threatened Bhopal, amidst the confusion which at this period prevailed in Central India, Luckma Dada, one of Sindiah's independent leaders was called upon as an auxiliary, and promised high pay and reward if he would recover the Fort of Hoshungabad, which had, immediately after the death of Chutta Khan, been attacked and taken by Ragojee Bhonslah, whose armies, aided by large bodies of Pindarries, had begun to lay waste the territories of Bhopal.

While these events threatened the destruction of this state, a person made his appearance as its defender, in a manner which gives to his history an air of romance which continued to its close. He came to the gate of the city, habited as a soldier of fortune, and attended by some well-mounted adherents, and on being stopped by the guard, proclaimed himself to be *Vizier Mahomed*, the son of Sheriff Mahomed Khan, the cousin of the reigning Nuwab (Hiyat Mahomed Khan), with whom he desired an interview. This was instantly granted. The Nuwab, after the first salutation, asked him how he had subsisted during his absence from Bhopal. He frankly avowed that, having been banished from his native country by the power of Chutta Khan, against whose administration his father had rebelled, he had been compelled to earn his livelihood by serving Huttee Singh, a plundering Rajpoot chief in the province of Omutwarra (21). He had learnt, he said, the profession of a soldier; and the reports which he heard of the distress and danger of the land of his ancestors, had made him determine, at all hazards, to offer his services, and to give his life (it was all he had), in any way the Nuwab pleased, for his country. The old prince was roused from his usual state of abstraction by the occurrence. He gave to Vizier Mahomed the endearing title of son, and hailed him (with a spirit of prophecy) as the future saviour of the state.

1799 The period was one of action. The troops of Nagpoor were besieging Hoshungabad, and the depredations of the Pindarries

(21) Omutwarra between 24° and 25° north latitude. *Malcolm*, p. 374, (A. D. 1798,) says, "a *youth* made his appearance," &c. *Vizier Mahomed* must have been at least 30 years old then.

were every day more dreadful. We may imagine how rapidly the fame of Vizier Mahomed, who at once became a distinguished actor in these scenes, increased, when we are told, in eight months after he reached Bhopal he was a popular candidate for the office of Dewan. The Nuwab is said to have determined on his elevation; but it was opposed by his son, Ghous Mahomed, and the mother of that prince, who represented the danger of giving such a station to a person whose mind was still warm with the wrongs of his family, and who had a father's death to revenge. It is to be regretted that Vizier Mahomed was not made Dewan, after he had proved himself so worthy of that station; for the Dewan who was appointed, was connected with Sultan Mahomed Khan's family, which had, when Byjeeram was Minister, been precluded from any interference with the management of the Bhopal territory.

It was acknowledged, however, that a Puthan of high rank was necessary to the conduct of affairs, and the choice, unfortunately, fell on Mooreed Mahomed Khan, the descendant of Sultan Mahomed Khan, (22) an hereditary lord of Rathgurh. This chief refused to accept the office till the Mahrattah auxiliaries were dismissed. A large sum of money

(22) Who was youngest son of Dost Mahomed Khan (the founder of Bhopal), and younger brother of Yar Mahomed Khan.

was given them in consequence of their agreeing to depart; and the new Dewan came, accompanied by a thousand adherents, to take charge of the Government. Mooreed Mahomed Khan, presented in his appearance and character a very remarkable contrast to Vizier Mahomed. He had more the look and manners of a Hindoo merchant, than an Affghan chief. On the first day of his arrival he encamped at the garden of his grand-father, Sultan Mahomed Khan, where the day was passed in a display of tender feelings. He wept aloud at the recollections of the misfortunes of his family, which this spot brought to his mind, and embraced the trees which had been planted by his dear ancestors. (23) Next day, when he was introduced to the old Nuwab, he addressed him in the most humble and fulsome language, calling him his more than father; he lavished at the same time the most exaggerated praise on Ghous Mahomed. The Beebee, at whose court he next attended, was termed his aunt, and the person towards whom he looked for advancement. A still more extraordinary part was acted when the chief bankers and merchants of the city waited upon him. He refused their usual offerings of money, and made them presents of clothes, and honored some of the principal

(23) Persian Manuscript.

with the titles of relations (24) All the citizens he met were conciliated by the most soothing language; and, to gratify the poorer classes, he directed considerable sums of money to be distributed in charity. Many of the inhabitants of Bhopal were delighted by a demeanor to which they had been so little accustomed; but the haughty and turbulent Affghan lords of that city could hardly repress their indignation at a conduct which they considered derogatory and disgraceful. Some, better acquainted with the individual by whom these acts were practised, waited anxiously till the veil should be withdrawn, and his real character developed. They were not long in suspense; for in less than a month the vindictive and avaricious spirit which Mooreed Mahomed Khan evinced, in the oppression of the aged widow of Rajah Byjeeram, opened the eyes of all. His conduct on this occasion was the more despicable, from the distressed condition the poor woman had been before reduced to. His next attack was on the late Dewan, Rajah Himmut Row, whom with his nephew, Khealee Ram, (25)

(24) Dherm Chund and Kool Chund were both styled cousins by this cajoling minister. The whole proceedings of this period are taken from authentic manuscripts, and from the statements of actors in the scenes described

(25) Sir John Malcolm says, "this person has been in my service for the last two years (1830-1831) He is a man of very clear intellect and has a complete knowledge of the affairs of Bhopal at this period."

the manager of Bersiah, he confined for six weeks, till they paid a fine of 10,000 rupees. The supplies extorted from such sources of petty oppression were insufficient either to satisfy the Dewan's avarice, or the wants of the state, which latter every day became more pressing, from the general confusion that prevailed throughout the whole of Central India.

The Bhopal possessions, in common with others, were now overrun by freebooters and robbers of every description, and the troops it was necessary to maintain for their defence, were clamorous for their pay. To relieve these wants, Mooreed Mahomed Khan, imposed a tax on each house in Bhopal, which was levied according to the real, or supposed, wealth of the inhabitants; and those whom he had a short time before conciliated by the most endearing epithets, were now treated with marked severity. Grown bold with success, the Dewan demanded money from the Beebee, and, irritated by her refusal, he determined on her destruction. (26) This lady though not married to Hiyat Mahomed Khan, had enjoyed, as his favorite mistress, all the rank and power of the first princesses. She paid little atten-

(26) Mooreed Mahomed Khan had persuaded the Nuwab and Ghous Mahomed to forbid any person attending durbar with their arms. This order induced Vizier Mahomed and other Pathans to retire from court, such an unusual order was a warning to all!

tion to the Nuwab, who was absorbed in religious contemplation ; which disqualified him for the management of the affairs of the principality.

Mooreed Mahomed, after exciting the prejudices of the Puthans against her, took the opportunity of a visit of ceremony to have her assassinated. Two of her principal officers were killed in her defence ; and though she fled from the court where she was seated to the inner apartments, the partisans of Mooreed Mohamed followed and dispatched her. The secret motives of the minister's conduct were soon revealed, by the plunder of all the property this lady had amassed ; a great part of which he is believed to have conveyed to Rathgurh, and other places, where, amid the rapid revolutions that ensued, it became lost to him and to the state.

The next person whom Mooreed Mahomed Khan, marked for destruction, was Vizier Mahomed, whose reputation excited both his jealousy and alarm ; but all his attempts against this young chief were unsuccessful. They added to the fame of the man whom he hated and dreaded. Vizier Mahomed, when sent with inadequate means to oppose the Pindarries, supplied, by his personal valor and judgment, the want of numbers, and obtained the admiration even of his enemies. Vizier Mahomed, when in the service of Huttee Singh, of Omutwarra, had, on a plundering expedition, the tail of his horse cut off completely. But, he knew his value too well to reject him on that account, and the fame of the horse, well known by this mark, and that of his rider, were associated It is asserted that the cry of "*Banda ghora ka Suwar,*" or the cavalier with the cut-tail horse, was certain to put the Pindarries to flight, whatever were their numbers. Vizier Mahomed's penetration soon developed the artifices of the Dewan, and he was cautioned not to trust himself in his power. A plan was laid by Mooreed Mahomed to cut him off near Cheynpoor Barree; but the letter which contained the instructions was intercepted and the Governor (Raheem Khan) of that place, to whom it was addressed, was defeated, and fled wounded, with the loss of guns and baggage, into his fort, which next day surrendered to Vizier Mahomed. The news of this was received by the timid Dewan as the prelude to his downfall, and regardless of every thing but personal safety and worldly consideration; he summoned to his aid a large body of Mahrattahs under Balaram Inglia (one of Dowlut Rao Sindiah's predatory leaders, who was then subsisting his force by pillage), and the standard of Sindiah was, on the arrival of this force, displayed over the ramparts of Futtygurh, and the citadel of Bhopal. The next concession the minister desired to make to his new allies, was the fort of Islamnuggur; but what his fears had granted, was saved by the spirit of an Affghan widow lady, named Motee Beebee (27), who, when the Mahrattahs were advancing, ordered the gates to be shut, and the guns to be opened, saying she knew not by what authority Mooreed Mahomed Khan, disposed of the Bhopal fortresses, and that she would not permit any strangers to intrude where she dwelt. The noble resolution of this high-minded female, appears to have been well supported by the troops of the garrison; and the Mahrattahs were forced to retire.

Vizier Mahomed, who had been employed in establishing his authority over the country round Cheynpoor Barree, moved, the moment he heard of this occurrence, upon Bhopal. This led the Dewan and his Mahrattah ally to march out of Futtygurh to a plain four miles distant, where they were re-inforced by some infantry and guns, and a body of troops under Bappoo Sindiah. The fort on this occasion was left to the care of the since celebrated Ameer Khan, to whom the custody of Ghous Mahomed was also assigned.

Vizier Mahomed had several sharp skirmishes with the Mahrattahs, in which his courage and talent gained him the advantage; but the numbers of his enemies would, perhaps, have ultimately prevailed, if the troubles

(27) Aunt to Vizier Mahomed.

which commenced in Sindiah's own possessions had not made him direct his leaders to withdraw from all interference with the affairs of Bhopal (28). These orders were immediately obeyed; but Balaram carried with him the Dewan, Mooreed Mahomed Khan, as far as Seronj. He now accused that chief of being the author of all his disappointments, and of being concerned in the resistance which had been made to his occupation of the fort of Islamnuggur. The other, in vain, denied the charge, and stated how irreconcilable such conduct was with his own interests; his notorious reputation as a deceiver, was brought forward by the Mahrattah leader in answer to all he could urge in his defence. He was threatened with torture, unless he immediately gave up the treasures he was known to possess, and his fears and confinement brought on a violent illness; but even this was treated as a trick, and when he died, Balaram refused for two days to allow his body to be buried, declaring his conviction that he had counterfeited death to effect his escape; nor was it till putrefaction had commenced, that the Mahrattah chief would resign his prey, and believe that for once, Mooreed Mahomed Khan did not practise deceit! The name of this man is doomed to execration by his tribe,

(28) The contest between Sindiah and the widows of his uncle and predecessor, commenced at this period.

and to this day, when a Puthan of Bhopal visits Seronj to pay his devotion at a shrine sacred to Murtiza Ali (29), it is deemed an essential part of the pilgrimage, to bestow five blows with a slipper on the tomb of Mooreed Mahomed Khan; to mark at once the contempt and indignation which his memory excites. It is obvious that there was a fundamental objection to the appointment of Mooreed Mahomed to be the Vizier, as his family had been, by agreement, excluded from a y interference in the management of the Bhop ' territory; whereas he was allowed to hold the chief post in the state. His character, too, must have been before known, or suspected. Vizier Mahomed was in 1798, when he came to offer his services to the Nuwab, about 33 years of age (30), and had proved by his character and conduct, that he merited, and he alone, the office of Minister. The result affords a dearly bought lesson to native Governments, and proves a want of wisdom in rejecting his claims, and the appointment to the office of Dewan, a man whose habits of business and character were not known: while Vizier Mahomed was cousin to the reigning Nuwab of Bhopal; and against whose appointment there existed no valid objection.

(29) This is the title by which the Caliph Ali, the nephew and son-in-law of the prophet Mahomed, is distinguished.

(30) He died in February, 1816, aged 51 years.

After the retreat of the Mahrattahs, Vizier Mahomed surrounded the fort of Futtygurh, of which Ameer Khan still retained possession. The latter, however, soon agreed to give up Ghous Mahomed, and to evacuate the place. He afterwards entered into the service of Bhopal, but was found so intriguing a character, that at the end of six months he was discharged; and proceeded to share the fortunes of Juswunt Row Holkar.

1802. The mode in which the revenues of Bhopal were collected, has been already noticed. The Dewan, which office Vizier Mahomed now filled, received all the collections, except those appropriated for the personal support of the Nuwab; but this revenue, from the distracted state of Malwa, and the incessant incursions of the Mahrattahs and Pindarries, was at the present period, not above 50,000 rupees (31), out of which an army was to be maintained, that could not be reduced below 4,000 men without endangering even the nominal sovereignty of a country, which it was always hoped might yet enjoy peace and prosperity. Under such circumstances, Vizier Mahomed cannot be censured for having, to preserve the existence of the state he governed, had recourse to the same irregular practices, to which all others, from Dowlut Rao Sindiah

(31) Sir John Malcolm gives this sum. It could only be meant of the *town* of Bhopal.

down to the pettiest chief in central India, then resorted; or in other words, to endeavour to make his army support itself. This system of indiscriminate violence, which appears on the first view to confound all rights and property, and to attain its ends by any expedient, was, nevertheless, not without its distinctions; certain principles being recognized, and, generally speaking, well observed by all parties.

The Bheels and other tribes of petty robbers, plundered wherever they could. The chiefs of the Pindarries often contracted obligations with the principal sovereigns of the country, which limited their depredations; and though these freebooters had never established any character for good faith or honor, they had a knowledge of their own interests which constituted some check on their proceedings. The Grassiah, or Rajpoot chiefs, who, deprived of their lands by the Mahrattahs still claimed a share of their revenues, on the ground of their ability to injure them, were satisfied with a fixed or known Tunkhwah, or tribute from certain territories, on which they had a real or pretended claim; and their irruptions were directed to enforce this payment The latter class of freebooters were always natives of the soil, and generally the friends, often the relations, of the zemindars, or landholders. Their war was with the government, not with the inhabitants. The next and highest description of plunderers were the existing governments. The armies and detachments of Dowlut Rao Sindiah, Holkar, and other Mahrattahs, wherever they marched, levied as heavy a contribution (32) as could be extorted from the managing officers of the province or town they entered or attacked. At this period the greatest part of the revenues of central India was collected in the manner described. The Cumpoos, or brigades, of Sindiah and of Holkar, traversed that unfortunate country, making little distinction to whom the place belonged, from which they desired to obtain money. The leaders of these corps had always the ready excuse, if they desired it, of a mutiny among their troops for arrears of pay; and the prince whose name they usurped, avowed or disapproved their actions, as it suited his temporary interests.

1803. Vizier Mahomed, not satisfied with the reconquest of the districts which had been taken from Bhopal, levied contributions on other states. He displayed equal gallantry and judgment in the various incursions he made into the neighbouring principalities, which he compelled to furnish a portion of revenue to supply his

(32) The districts of Raiseen, Ashta, Sehore, Duraha, and Itchawar, were reconquered, and contributions were levied from Shujahalpoor, Bersiah, Bhilsa, on the north side of the Nerbuddah, and from Seonee, and other districts south of that river.

exhausted resources. But of all his exploits, there is none during this period of his life which reflects more credit on his character as a soldier, than the recapture of Hoshungabad, which he, in concert with the Pindarries, came upon suddenly, and with such determined resolution, that he actually terrified its governor into a surrender (33). After this exploit, Vizier Mahomed carried on for several years a petty warfare, marked by vicissitudes, with the Mahrattah chiefs, who now considered him as a declared enemy. He, in consequence, endeavoured to strengthen himself by a connexion with the Pindarries. His first ally among the freebooters was Kurreem Khan, to whom he gave two villages in Bersiah. Cheetoo, another Pindarry chief, entered also into

(33) This event occurred in 1803. About a year after the reduction of Raiseen, Hoshungabad had capitulated to the Nagpoor Rajah in 1799, and remained with him till thus recaptured The Marquess of Wellesley, Despatches, A D. 1837, vol. 4, p. 407, 24th March, 1850, to the Secret Committee writes, " About ten years ago the Rajah of Berar obtained possession of that fort by the treachery of the persons to whose charge it was committed, but shortly before the conclusion of peace between the British Government and the Rajah of Berar, the Nuwab of Bhopal, taking advantage of the adverse condition of the Rajah of Berar's affairs, recovered the fort and territory of Hoshungabad, and has since retained possession against the efforts of a considerable force of the Rajah of Berar." Peace was concluded with the Berar Rajah on the 17th of December, 1803, and with Sindiah on the 30th December, 1803, after the battle of Argaum. Despatches, vol. 3, Appendix B and C. pp 633, 634. The Marquess would make the capture by the Berar Rajah about the year 1795.—Malcolm, p. 386, gives the year 1798.

a compact of friendship with the prince of Bhopal. He was promised a place of refuge for his family in one of the fortresses, and received a grant of the village of Chippaneer on the Nerbuddah. This Pindarry leader, in return, aided the state of Bhopal against the Rajah of Nagpoor.

The relations between the state of Bhopal and the government of Sindiah had latterly undergone a considerable change, of which it is here necessary to take a retrospect. Madhojee Sindiah had been throughout his life, looked upon as the friendly protector of the Affghan principality; and though an actual supremacy was either asserted or admitted, still, there was, from the policy of both parties, an implied connexion. This led to considerable importance being attached to the Khillut, or ordinary dresses, which Dowlut Rao Sindiah sent to the Nuwab, and to Vizier Mahomed Khan; but, the latter, nevertheless, kept aloof when Sindiah required him to accompany his army, then on its march to attack Juswunt Rao Holkar. The consequence of this caution was, that when the Pindarry leaders, Kurreem Khan, Dost Mahomed, and Cheetoo, were loaded with favors and created Nuwabs for the Mahrattah ruler now conferred this Mahomedan title (34), in consideration of the

(34) "The bestowing this title had no form, but the chiefs, Sindiah or Holkar, addressing the favored person in writing, or

aid they had given, the brother of Vizier Mahomed, whom he sent to congratulate that prince on his success, was received with such marked coolness, as left little doubt of the measures in contemplation.

1804. It has been before stated (1802) that Ameer Khan had entered into the service of Bhôpal, but being found a very intriguing character, was discharged at the end of six months. It appears from the depositions of some of the prisoners taken at Mahoba in Bundelkund, by the force under Lieut.-Colonel Martindell, on the 2nd of July, 1804, that Meer Khan was at that period of time "engaged in hostile operations against the Nuwab of Bhopal;" (35) on the 29th of December, 1804, the acting Resident at Dowlut Rao Sindiah's court wrote as follows to the Marquess of Wellesley (36) "the preparations for active measures, which are still in train in this army, notwithstanding the assurances I have received of the intention of Dowlut Rao Sindiah to proceed to his capital (37), appear to me

verbally, as Nuwab; on which the Chobdars or Durbar officers, proclaimed the new title, and the party ever after assumed it, was addressed by it in letters, and had it engraved on his seal. Sindiah had no title to make Nuwabs. The right existed in the Emperor of Delhi. After the last Mahrattah War (1817-18) the British Government made Ameer Khan, a Nuwab.

(35) The Marquess of Wellesley's Despatches, vol. 5, p. 143, Supplement Mahrattah War, Letter of the Governer General in Council, No. 2, dated 24th March 1805, to the Secret Committee.

(36) Ditto, p. 132. (37) Oujeen.

to manifest an unequivocal spirit of hostility. My demand for the dismissal of Ghautka (38) has not been complied with, while the army of Dowlut Rao Sindiah is daily recruited with fresh levies, and the situation of the armies of Baptiste at *Bhopal*, of Meer Khan at Bhilsa, and of other chiefs in Malwa, combined with the notoriety of the inimical counsels still in agitation at this court, indicate, in my judgment, a decided intention on the part of Sindiah to commence hostilities at an early period; I have, therefore, signified my resolution of quitting camp should arrangements not be immediately adopted to convince me of a contrary spirit, and I shall deem it to be my duty to carry my design into execution (39), unless the conduct to be instantly pursued by Sindiah, shall be perfectly satisfactory to my mind."

1805. This year Sindiah and the Berar Rajah, after the Mahrattah war had been terminated, were desirous of attacking the Bhopal state. Sir John *Malcolm*, as before observ-

(38) Father-in-law to Sindiah. Ghautka was the chief adviser of all these hostile movements.

(39) The conduct of Sindiah was very improper on this occasion. He would not permit Mr. (now Sir R) Jenkins to quit his camp. It is usual for residents, as well as for ambassadors, at Native or European courts, to quit them when war is determined on, or amicable relations have ceased The detention was, alone, a national insult, and a valid ground for a declaration of war

ed, states that there was "*an implied connexion*" between Sindiah and the Nuwab of Bhopal. Major General the Hon'ble Sir Arthur *Wellesley*, in a letter to Colonel Barry *Close*, dated 4th March, 1805, (40) writes, "There can be no doubt that the conduct of Sindiah throughout has been very improper, but not, in my opinion, in making an attack upon Bhopal or Saugur. There is no doubt but that he had a claim upon the Nuwab of Bhopal, and it is more than probable that he had one upon Saugur, which, as you observe, holds but very slightly on the Peshwah: but his misbehaviour has been, in my opinion, principally towards Mr. *Jenkins*." (41). The Marquess of Wellesley and council, in their letter, dated 24th March, 1805, to the Secret Committee of the Hon'ble Court of Directors, write (42) "that the resident, Mr. *Jenkins*, told Sindiah that an attack upon the independent territory of Bhopal was contrary to the provisions of the subsidiary treaty," and that "the Nuwab of Bhopal had maintained the relations of amity and peace both with Dowlut Rao Sindiah and the British Government," that Dowlat Rao Sindiah began by justifying his conduct towards the Nuwab of Bhopal, by asserting that the Nuwab of Bhopal was a tributary to his Govern-

(40) The Duke of Wellington's Despatches, vol. 2, p. 596.
(41) The detention of Mr Jenkins.
(42) Despatches, vol. 4, p. 419.

ment." Dowlut Rao, also told the Resident that "the design of His Highness was, by levying contributions from the Nuwab of that territory, to place his army in a condition to act with effect against the enemy." (43) The Resident, in his remarks upon Sindiah's conduct writes, "The Nuwab of Bhopal is not a tributary state to Sindiah, so considered, although it is true that he has been subjected to such exactions as the superior force of Sindiah has occasionally rendered it convenient for him to enforce; but, the true object of Sindiah's march to this place was founded on a plan concerted between him and the Rajah of Nagpoor, for the purpose of assisting Raghojee Bhonslah (44), in wresting the fort and territory of Hoshungabad from the Nuwab of Bhopal. This plan has long been mentioned as an object of notoriety, but I did not consider myself at liberty to make a formal representation on the subject, either to the Durbar or to your Excellency; but I have this morning been furnished with such proofs as leave no doubt of the fact in my mind, and I am accordingly informed, that the troops of Nagpoor, stationed at the distance of about 30 coss from Hoshungabad, have been ordered to resume their march towards that place, since

(43) Holkar and Meer Khan are here supposed to be meant, by Sindiah · but the British Government was evidently intended.

(44) Rajah of Berar.

the invasion of the Bhopal territories by Dowlut Rao Sindiah." The Resident adds—"this violation of his engagements (45), by Dowlut Rao Sindiah, appears to me to be the more aggravated at the present crisis, as its obvious consequence is to detach from the objects of the war against Holkar, whatever power the Maharajah may be supposed to command, as well as to augment the number of our enemies; by precipitating the Nuwab of Bhopal into an intimate alliance with Meer Khan."

The Marquess of Wellesley further writes to the Secret Committee, (46) "the Minister (47) then proceeded to state that Hylut Rao had brought a letter from Meer Khan, purporting that he (Meer Khan) was prepared to oppose any attempt on the part of the Rajah of Berar to molest the territory of the Nuwab of Bhopal. The Minister added that the Rajah had nevertheless determined to prosecute the expedition against Hoshungabad, and that Saccaram Bukshee, the Rajah's principal military officer, had taken the field with that intention."

It is obvious that there never was any solicitation on the part of the Nuwab of Bhopal

(45) Which Mr Jenkins considered as a breach of the 8th article of the treaty of defensive alliance, "by negotiating with the Rajah of Nagpoor, without giving previous notice and mutual consultation with the British Government."

(46) Page 434

(47) Of the Rajah of Berar, speaking to the Resident

to be placed under the protection of Sindiah; what Sir J. *Malcolm* means by an "*implied connexion*," it is difficult to understand, as he, at the same time, states (48) that "no *actual* supremacy was either asserted or *admitted.* It is true, though, that, in the year 1798, (49) Himmut Rao, the Minister of Bhopal, to avert the dangers which threatened Bhopal, amidst the confusion which at this time prevailed in Central India, invited Luckma Dada, one of Sindiah's independent leaders; who was called upon as an auxiliary, and promised high pay and reward if he would recover the fort of Hoshungabad, which had been taken by the Rajah of Berar This was no application made to *Sindiah,* but to one of his "*independent* leaders." The Marquess of Wellesley writes, (50) "The possession of the fort of Hoshungabad with its dependent territory, which belongs to the Nuwab of Bhopal, has uniformly been an object of the Rajah of Berar's desire, and his endeavours to obtain and secure that possession, have occasioned repeated contests between those chieftains." Vizier Mahomed had recovered the fort, and it is clear that he would not have applied direct to Sindiah, whose connexion with the Rajah of Berar must have been suspected. Hence the minister applied to an independent

(48) Page 387. (49) Page 373.
(50) Despatches, vol. 4, p. 407.

chief: and it is difficult to imagine, how any such act could render an *independent*, a *dependent* state! Major General Wellesley no doubt wrote under the belief that Sindiah had a claim on Bhopal, but he states no reason. He writes, "There is no doubt but that he (Sindiah) had a claim upon the Nuwab of Bhôpal." Sindiah, too, only made the assertion. There was no proof of any tribute paid, or ever promised. Sindiah, as the stronger power, could send a force and extort money. The Berar Rajah might have done the same: so that Bhopal might have been liable to pay a forced tribute to both! The fact is, that the relations between Sindiah and the other Mahrattahs with the states in Central India, were then little known.

The Marquess of Wellesley states that the Nuwab of Bhopal, fearing the hostility of Sindiah, and of the Rajah of Berar, was desirous of placing himself under the protection of the British Government. He writes in the above quoted letter that—"An Agent (51) from the Nuwab of Bhopal arrived in the camp of Dowlut Rao Sindiah, with letters from the Nuwab, addressed to the Hon'ble Major Genl. Wellesley, and to the British Resident of Dowlut Rao Sindiah's court. The object of this mission appeared to be founded on a report, that in consideration of a sum of money, Dow-

(51) Enayet Musseah

lut Rao Sindiah was disposed to grant military aid to the Rajah of Berar, for the recovery of the fort and territory of Hoshungabad ; and under an apprehension that Dowlut Rao Sindiah might he aided in the prosecution of that measure by the British troops, the Nuwab of Bhopal signified to the Resident, through the channel of his agent, his desire of placing himself under the protection of the British Government, on the foundation of the engagement formerly concluded by him (52) with Brigr. Genl. *Goddard* (53). To this overture the Resident replied in terms of civility, by explaining those principles of British policy which preclude the interposition of our power to aid the purposes of conquest, or to influence the result of any contest between states with which the British Government is connected by the ties of amity" The Marquess also writes (54)—" It was obvious at the same time, that the march of Sindiah with his army to Hoshungabad, was favourable to the renewal of a confederacy between the Rajah of Berar and Dowlut Rao Sindiah, especially under the actual existence of circumstances which had a tendency to that effect." And (55) " on the

(52) Hiyat Mahomed Khan was the Nuwab.

(53) It is a pity that the proceedings of the force under the General should have been kept at Bombay Sir J Malcolm does not mention any " engagement," but it is highly probable that future protection was solicited, and considered as promised.

(54) Vol. 4, p. 414. (55) Page 419.

Resident's arrival in camp, Dowlut Rao Sindiah's army was in motion to invade the territory of Bhopal. The Resident followed Dowlut Rao Sindiah to Seonee, a small fortified village within the territory of Bhopal, which his troops were employed in attacking under the conduct of Serje Rao Gautka (56). The Resident remarked to Sindiah—"That this procedure constituted a violation of the principles of the defensive alliance, which were directly adverse to aggressive war and conquest. That an attack, therefore, upon the independent territory of Bhopal was contrary to the provisions of the subsidiary treaty."

It was obvious, that the intention was to make a joint attack on Bhopal, and that having reduced it, the Berar Rajah and Dowlut Rao Sindiah, would have been strengthened by the event; after which, Holkar and Meer Khan (57) would have joined the confederacy, in an attack upon the British. It was, therefore, desirable to prevent Sindiah joining the Berar Rajah; and, thus, the general policy of the British Government insured, indirectly, "protection to Bhopal; for its destruction would have strengthened the power of the Mahrattahs in Central India; after a long war had been waged by the British Government

(56) The chief hostile adviser, and Sindiah's father-in-law.

(57) I have before shown that in 1804, Meer Khan did make an attack on the Bhopal territory.

in Upper Hindoostan, and in the South of India, to curtail their power and means of aggression. In the unsettled state of the British newly acquired territories, the Government did not desire to do more than prescribe to Sindiah and the Rajah of Berar, upon general principles, a non-aggressive system of conduct. The noble and disinterested conduct of the Nuwab of Bhopal towards General *Goddard's* army, had earned the protection which it solicited. The state of Sindiah's and the Berar Rajah's relations in Central India, appear to have been imperfectly known. At the same time it is clear, as a general policy, that it is advisable to protect smaller states against the greater: for, otherwise, the lesser would be absorbed by the greater powers

1806. Ghous Mahomed, the son of the nominal Nuwab, continued to regard Vizier Mahomed after his elevation to the office of Dewan, with envy and hatred, and in consequence entered into a league with the Pindarry chief, Kurreem Khan, to support his authority (58). Their first efforts were so far successful, as to compel Vizier Mahomed to retire from Bhopal; but, he soon returned, and drawing them from that capital, forced them to seek refuge in the camp of Dowlut Rao Sindiah, who was then engaged in the siege of a neighbouring fortress. Although that prince deemed this

(58) Malcolm, p. 388.

the proper period to execute a design he had long cherished, of seizing Kurreem Khan (59), yet it did not prevent his listening to the complaints of Ghous Mahomed Khan; and so eager was this prince to ruin Vizier Mahomed, that he engaged to surrender the fort of Islamnuggur, pay four lakhs of rupees in cash, and present an annual tribute (60) of 50,000 to Sindiah, with 11,000 rupees to his public officers. Having consented to these terms, he proceeded to Bhopal, after being invested with an honorary dress by Dowlut Rao Sindiah, whose ostensible support he seems to have thought sufficient to maintain him in power; nor does he appear to have met with any opposition on the part of Vizier Mahomed. But what could Vizier Mahomed do while the Nuwab was alive, and the son was permitted to exercise the powers of Nuwab: and the minister had not always possessed the full executive authority.

The result, however, proves that while it was incompatible with the views of the British Government at the time to take Bhopal under its protection, it, unfortunately led to that state seeking support from Sindiah; a measure, could it have been foreseen, it would have been good policy to have prevented. In the com-

(59) This occurred in A. D. 1806, Sindiah afterwards proceeded to besiege Rathgurh, which was evacuated.

(60) The first mention of tribute in any work, or document!

plicated interests which absorbed the mind of the Governor General, and in the absence of real information as to the state of Central India, the Marquess of Wellesley was, no doubt, anxious not to embroil the Government in another war; and perhaps, too much credence may have been given to the declaration of Sindiah, that Bhopal was a state tributary to him. From the period of General *Goddard's* force being in that part of India, till the year 1805, Central India was little known; the interests of various states being so mixed up with the great Mahrattah Powers. It, also, proves that a great error was committed in not, at first, appointing Vizier Mahomed, Dewan, instead of Mooreed Mahomed; but, when his oppressive conduct became known by such positive proofs, he should have been displaced, and Vizier Mahomed have been the Minister: and his noble conduct, merited all confidence.

Consequent upon the above agreement with Sindiah, the fort of Islamnuggur was immediately surrendered to one of Sindiah's officers; and 18 days after that event Hiyat Mahomed Khan, the Nuwab, died. He was 73 years of age, very corpulent, and of large stature This prince was completely exhausted by the harrassing scenes amid which he lived; and those near him relate that his invocations for death to release him were frequent and earnest. In the same year that Hiyat Mahomed died, Hoshungabad and Cheynpoor Barree were taken by the armies of the Nagpoor Rajah, one of whose generals, Sadick Ali, was invited by Ghous Mahomed to advance on Bhopal. Vizier Mahomed probably felt himself unable to prevent these ruinous measures, taken as they were by one who was the recognized Prince of the country. Vizier Mahomed in consequence, retired to the fortress of Gunnour, leaving the capital, and part of his own property, to be plundered. Sadick Ali, after remaining at Bhopal about six weeks, retired towards Nagpoor, carrying with him the son of Ghous Mahomed, as a hostage, while the agents left in possession of Bhopal, placed that Prince under restraint. It was a desperate crisis of affairs, when Vizier Mahomed beheld his native country so near destruction by such powerful enemies: but, it will be seen that Vizier Mahomed triumphed over his enemies.

1807. Sindiah this year besieged Rathgurh, which fort was evacuated. Vizier Mahomed watched these events, and encouraged by the security that appeared to reign among his enemies, he determined on an attempt to recover Bhopal. He left Gunnour with his adherents in the evening, and by break of day reached the city; (61) the walls were instantly assaulted, the Mahrattahs in the town were attacked and expelled, and the fort of Futtygurh was

(61) A distance of nearly 40 miles.

evacuated during the night Ghous Mahomed and Vizier Mahomed met the next morning, when the Nuwab declared that he had been betrayed by wicked men, whom he named. Vizier Mahomed ordered them to be immediately produced, saying. "If these are the wretches who have betrayed you, punish them forthwith." Six Hindoo officers of rank, or more, were put to death. (62) Besides these, two brahmins were bound; and a cow being killed before them, the blood was poured down their throats; they were then liberated, and desired to go and describe the taste of cow's blood to Sindiah and the Nagpoor Rajah. It was thought that he had outraged the feelings of the Mahrattah princes, of whom the traitors whom he punished were but the instruments, beyond the hope of forgiveness; (63) but he succeeded for the moment, in averting the anger of Sindiah, by promising faithfully to fulfil the terms into which Ghous Mahomed had entered, and by sending his eldest son (64), as a hostage for the liquidation of such part of

(62) Lal Jee and Roop Chund were trodden to death by elephants. Nowlut Rae Lal, Bukshee (or Pay Master), Benee Lal, Moonshee (Secretary), and Sooruj Mull, were blown from guns *Malcolm*, p. 391.

(63) Both Sindiah and the Nagpoor Rajah would have treated any Mahomedans in a manner most degrading to their religious prejudices. It was not an act committed from a religious feeling—but the punishment of treason: on which occasions, torture is often resorted to.

(64) Ameer Mahomed Khan.

the four lakhs of rupees as was still in arrear. Nothing but the determined conduct of Vizier Mahomed, at this crisis, saved the Bhopal principality: for, otherwise, Sindiah and the Nagpoor Rajah would have divided the principality between them; and, thus strengthened, they would have thrown into confusion the whole of Central India: and, then, would the Mahrattah War of 1817-1818, have been anticipated.

1808. "About a year after the above transactions, Vizier Mahomed reconquered the territories of Bhopal north of the Nerbuddah, which had been seized by Sadick Ali, (65) whose brother, the governor of those districts, was slain. Some months afterwards, Ameer Khan solicited and obtained the assistance of Vizier Mahomed in a contest with the Rajah of Nagpoor. They came upon the troops of that prince in a situation where they were strongly posted; but Ameer Khan, nevertheless, proposed an immediate attack. Vizier Mahomed, who was remarkable, notwithstanding his sense and courage, for his superstitious prejudices, (66) said the day was unfortunate, and

(65) The Nagpoor Rajah's General.

(66) "He always carried about him a Tuqweem, or Almanack, in which the good and bad days were noted, according to the calculations of astrologers; but besides this he had great faith in omens. It is difficult to say, how much of this belief was real or pretended; he certainly, amidst the extraordinary vicissitudes of his life, often derived, and imparted to his followers, courage from the slightest events."

requested him to defer it. This, however, Ameer Khan refused to do, with an expressed contempt of the reason on which the advice was grounded. The action, in which he immediately engaged, had an unfavorable termination. Ameer Khan being (from having fallen from his horse) reported slain, his followers, after plundering their own camp, fled in every direction. The discomfited chief went to the tent of Vizier Mahomed, who had taken no share in the battle, and requested he would accompany him in the retreat he was compelled to make. But Vizier Mahomed, who was disgusted with the whole conduct of his ally, and quite indignant at the cowardice and want of discipline of his followers, bade Ameer Khan go back, as he had advanced, alone. "You," he said, "who have no country to fight for, may think a casual defeat of little importance; but, in the defence of a state, the reputation of its leader is one of its strongest bulwarks; and that, if once lost, cannot be regained; what hopes could a people entertain of a chief in my situation, who shrunk from danger? Retreat, therefore, shall never be resorted to by me, till I have convinced my enemies that I am resolved to achieve whatever is within the range of possibility." (67) This conference

(67) Malcolm says, "I took down this speech of Vizier Mahomed from the relation of a most intelligent native, who was present when it was made; and had it subsequently confirmed by others who heard it."

was quite public. Vizier Mahomed acted as he said he would; he immediately led his troops, who were animated by his brave resolution, and proud of the superiority of their chief, against the Nagpoor army, which he forced, in their turn, to give ground; but their numbers were too great, and he derived no benefit from his attack, except the substantial one of maintaining his high name by this temporary success." It is by such men as Vizier Mahomed, that kingdoms have been conquered or recovered. Had such a chief accompanied the Emperor, Shah Allum, to Delhi, when he went to ascend his throne: he never would have been a captive King in the hands of the Mahrattahs.

1809. Vizier Mahomed's attempts, at this period, to obtain the assistance and mediation of the British Government, were again unsuccessful; (68) "for though there was no doubt, from the character of Vizier Mahomed, that it was with a view to self-preservation alone that he had contracted friendship with the Pindarry leaders and with Ameer Khan, this could not prevent his being classed among those who had combined to overrun the territories of Nagpoor and the Dekhan. He had, in fact, not only co-operated with these plunderers,

(68) Malcolm, p. 394. Enayet Musseah was employed on this occasion to endeavour to interest Mr. Jenkins, the resident at the court of Nagpoor, in his favor.

but his country was their professed asylum He was, in consequence, at this period, in imminent hazard from the British forces, which advanced under Colonel Barry *Close* across the Nerbuddah (69). That army acted in co-operation with the Rajah of Nagpoor against Ameer Khan; but, Colonel *Close* had discretionary orders with regard to Bhopal.

(69) Vizier Mahomed had been compelled to call in the aid of certain Pindarry chiefs (chiefly Mahomedan leaders) when he found protection denied him from a higher quarter The unsettled state of Central India had allowed of the formation of Pindarry Durrahs, under various chiefs Sindiah and the other Mahrattahs were compelled to assign them villages, to save their own territories from plunder! When the Marquess of Hastings in 1817 took the field against the Pindarries, he had reason to know that either the Mahrattah powers would support the Pindarries, or that they could not put them down; which ever cause it may have been, it was the clear policy of the Governor General, to take the field with large divisions amounting altogether to 116,464 men, regulars and irregulars. If, therefore, it required such a force to put down about 20,000 Pindarries—rated at one time at 40,000—how could the Bhopal state, having been obliged to call them in, speedily get rid of them! Ameer Khan first aided Bhopal, then attacked its territory, and lastly solicited the assistance of Vizier Mahomed! Lieut.-Col. *Blacker*, Qr. Mr. General Madras army—Memoir of the Operations of the British Army in the Mahrattah War of 1817, 1818, and 1819—published in 1821, (quarto,) gives the British force (regulars) at 87,591, but with irregulars, at 116,464, p. 25, and 295 guns. At p. 19, he gives the forces of Sindiah, Holkar, Peshwah, Bhonslah, Ameer Khan, Nizam, and Pindarries, at 217,332 men and 589 guns: of this force he puts down the Pindarries 16,500, and 20 guns

At p. 18 he states that Captain *Sydenham*, Political Agent in Berar, estimated them, in 1814, at 20,000 and 18 guns. one half of them considered fit for military service, and the rest for the work of devastation and plunder. Lieut.-Col. *Adams*, in July, 1817, estimated them at 20,000 horse and foot, and 22 guns.

The court of Nagpoor was jealous of British interference, as Sindiah had been on a former occasion. The manly and open conduct of Vizier Mahomed, dispelled all doubt as to the character of his connexion with the Pindarries; while Sadick Ali (70) was siezing Cheynpoor Barree and other possessions, Vizier Mahomed sent an agent to Colonel *Close*, to describe the necessity under which he had acted; to urge, a third time, the claims of the Bhopal family on the British nation, for the aid formerly given to General *Goddard;* and finally to state his complete acquiescence in whatever terms the Colonel might dictate. His agent was instructed to declare distinctly, that no thoughts of opposition were entertained against a nation, which was regarded by the Princes and nobles of Bhopal, with an hereditary feeling of hope and confidence; and towards which no extreme of distress could ever make them place themselves in the relation of enemies.

The conduct of Vizier Mahomed and his officers, when the British troops were within, or near, his territories, corresponded with his professions. The policy of Raghojee Bhonslah (of Nagpoor) was vacillating The British Government had every day less cause to rely on the friendship of its ally; who clearly was endeavouring to ruin the Bhopal state, under cover of the presence of a British force: and by its

(70) The Nagpoor Rajah's general.

presence to prevent resistance! This aggressive policy was contrary to the treaty existing between the Rajah and the British Government. Vizier Mahomed saw, and took advantage of this state of affairs: he eagerly pressed the claim of Bhopal to British protection; but an apprehension that interference in its concerns would involve much embarrassment, and carry the British Government beyond the limits within which they wished to confine themselves; led to the rejection of all the propositions which Vizier Mahomed then made, and often repeated, during the seven successive years of his arduous and unsupported struggles, to maintain the existence of the state of which he was the head. His not being able to obtain protection against his enemies, called forth those qualities of the statesman, and of the general, which flourish best in times of extreme difficulty and danger. But, though he proved successful, it was a dangerous alternative to be reduced to. No doubt a belief in his high destiny supported him on the trying occasion. In 1805, when protection was first solicited, the Marquess of *Wellesley*, Governor General of India, had very important political affairs to settle, at a period when he was about to leave India; and Central Indian politics were but little known. In 1808, and during the time the Earl of *Minto* was Governor General, an army was sent to the banks of the Sutlege to settle affairs with Runjeet Singh, the Sikh chief, who wished to subdue and annex to his dominions, the petty Sikh states lying to the south of the Sutlege; which, for a series of years, had been dependent on the empire of Delhi. These states claimed the protection of the British Government, which they received; hence they are called the "Protected Sikh States." Two expeditions were sent beyond sea to the Mauritius and to Java. (71) It was unfortunate that circumstances did prevent protection being afforded to Bhopal till a later period: for the services rendered by that state to General *Goddard* in 1778, were of paramount importance.

"Vizier Mahomed was at once an object of terror and of calumny at the Mahrattah courts, particularly at those of *Nagpoor* and *Gwalior*. Their efforts to destroy him, had driven him to have recourse to every means for the preservation of himself, and his country; but, forgetting that *they* were the *real authors* of the condition in which he was placed, they represented him as a willing associate of the Pindarries, the patron of plunderers; and the chief enemy to the restoration of peace in Central India. His being viewed in this light,

(71) The Goorkhas had, shortly after Lord Minto arrived in India, attacked the Police Thannahs on our frontier, in the Teraee: and satisfaction being refused, his Lordship was compelled, by the above circumstances, to leave to the Earl of Moira, a Nipal War.

created a combination of various states against him, which, from the strength collected, seemed to render his escape from destruction almost impossible. That he did baffle them all, evinces in a remarkable manner, what the Natives of India are capable of effecting, when commanded by an able leader, who possesses their confidence and attachment." Vizier Mahomed was fighting to preserve his country: the Mahrattahs to destroy it: and, here, right was victorious over the mighty efforts of his enemies.

1812. In March, 1812, one of Dowlut Rao Sindiah's principal generals, Juggoo Bappoo, made an attack on Bhopal, with the troops of which he had several slight actions, but appears to have made no impression. The pretence for this attack was the non-payment of a sum of money due by Vizier Mahomed to the government of Sindiah. On a small amount of money being given, and a promise of more, Juggoo Bappoo retired during the monsoon to a neighbouring district. After the rains, Juggoo Bappoo again advanced; and the approach of the Nagpoor troops under Sadick Ali; announced the commencement of that combined plan of operations, which Sindiah and the Rajah of Nagpoor had for some time contemplated against Bhopal. Their object was its *annihilation*, and an engagement was entered into, by which the confederates agreed to share equally, (72) the Bhopal territories: the complete conquest of which they anticipated, as the certain result of their great preparations.

The city of Bhopal, which stands on the high land of Gondwarra, north of the Nerbuddah, is of considerable extent, and about four miles in circumference. It is surrounded by a tolerable wall, but was then without any ditch or other defence, on three faces. On the other, or southern face, is the citadel of Futtygurh, which stands on an eminence, and is defended on one side by the tank, or lake, of Bhopal; a noble sheet of water, which extends in length five miles, and is in average breadth about one mile. Most of the irregular crags or heights upon the bank of the lake, had formerly been fortified; but all these works were, at this period, in a very bad condition, and their appearance, with that of the empty houses (for Vizier Mahomed had warned all the inhabitants who could not share in the toils and dangers of the siege, to depart), made Bhopal look more like a deserted ruin than the capital of a country. The following account was given to Sir John *Malcolm* by a respectable Mahomedan, named Ameer Khan, who had been a soldier, and had become a merchant. His written account

(72) This was the original intention of Sindiah and the Rajah of Nagpoor, in 1805.

was composed and corrected by those of several others, and no fact is stated that has not been authenticated. Ameer Khan witnessed the actions he described.

1813. Vizier Mahomed had within the walls of Bhopal nearly 6,000 horse and foot in his own pay, 3,000 Pindarries, under Namdar Khan, nephew of Kurreem Khan, and 2,000 men furnished by the zemindars of the Tal pergunnah, and by Ruttun Singh, Thakoor, or lord, of Satunbaree. (73) When Juggoo Bappoo (74), after the rainy season was over, invested Bhopal, he was joined by one of his officers named Dau Singh, who re-inforced him with 12 battalions of infantry and 30 guns; and this force, already amounting to 25,000 men, was subsequently augmented by the corps of Ram Lal and Krishna Bhow (75), consisting of 15,000 men, horse and foot, and an army from Nagpoor under Sadick Ali of nearly 30,000 men. When this great force, amounting altogether, it was said, to 70,000 men (76) was assembled, the siege commenc-

(73) The Bengal and Agra Gazetteer, vol. 2, part 2, p. 284, states, that at the commencement of the siege, the force did not exceed 8 or 10,000 men. This work was published under the authority of Lord Auckland, when Governor General.

(74) His proper name was Jugapah Bappoo, but he is best known in Indian history by the name of Juggoo Bappoo.

(75) Ram Lal, Commander of the Infantry, and Krishna Bhow of the Cavalry.

(76) Sir John Malcolm says, "perhaps exaggerated by 10 or

ed. During the first fortnight there was only a cannonading; after which the regular Infantry commanded by Dan Singh, assaulting Vizier Mahomed's out-posts, drove them, with much loss on both sides, under the shelter of the town, (77) whilst the besiegers began to batter—having occupied all the advanced positions from which the besieged had been driven. The latter, when confined within the walls, suffered some distress, particularly the Pindarries, who, representing to Vizier Mahomed that they were unable to procure forage for their horses, requested his permission to withdraw from the city. Vizier Mahomed consented, and the Pindarries withdrew by a by-road unknown to the enemy. Most of the mounted troops belonging to the zemindars were compelled, by the same necessity, to follow this example. Many promised, however, to assist as much as possible, by conveying grain to the town as opportunities should occur: they fulfilled their pledges, and the besieged received, for a time, occasional supplies by a secret road leading from the gates of the old fort of Bhopal, over hills and defiles. But a deserter from the town gave informa-

15,000 men—but acknowledged by all to have been very great." The Gazetteer, p. 233, says, "50 or 60,000 men."

(77) Major Henley, in his notes on this siege, states, "that the friends of Vizier Mahomed had the utmost difficulty in prevailing on him to abandon the tombs of his ancestors, where the principal battery of the enemy was afterwards raised."

tion to the enemy of this communication, and it was immediately stopped by Sadick Ali, who occupied a space reaching from the gate of the old fort, to the Gunnour gate of the town wall. Juggoo Bappoo also took positions which commanded the approach to the principal gates of the town wall; and the three or four remaining gates were blocked up in the same manner by Ram Lal and Krishna Bhow. Whilst the enemy were employed in preventing the ingress to or from the town, Vizier Mahomed made his dispositions for defence, by posting a certain number of men inside each gate, in the following manner.

The old fort was guarded by a Rajpoot officer, named Doongurh Singh, with 100 men. The Gunnour gate by Thakoor Jey Singh, with 200 men. The Gondwarra gate by a Syud named Meer Bakur Ali, with 200 men. The Mungulwarra by another Syud named Nunga Sir (bareheaded), from continually going with his head uncovered, who had 200 men under him. The Etwarra gate by Moolaeem Khan, with 200 men. The Jumarath gate by a Chelah named Khoja Buksh, with 200. The Soondwarra gate by Moiz Mahomed Khan, the son of Ghous Mahomed (the Nuwab), with 400 men; and the Hummamel gate by Kurreem Mahomed Khan, with 200. In a suburb, called Vizier-gunj, founded by Vizier Mahomed outside the town, an officer named Goolshun

Rao was posted with 500 men. Futtygurh was defended by an officer named Dil Mahomed Khan, with 200 men. A fortified eminence within Futtygurh, called the Bala Killa, or upper fort, was guarded by a Rajpoot, named Jalim Singh, with 100 men. The Sally-port of Futtygurh was defended by Soota Khan, a Chelah, with 100 men. Vizier Mahomed did not restrict himself to any particular place; but, with 500 men under his immediate personal command, had a general superintendence over all the posts, to any of which he was ready to move as occasion required. This was the disposal of 3,100 Infantry.

Vizier Mahomed gave a strict order to his troops that they should not expend ammunition by firing unnecessarily, which could only tend to impress the enemy with an opinion of their unsteadiness; and he was so rigid in enforcing its observance, that after the occurrence of several false alarms from unnecessary firing, he punished the offenders by cutting off their ears and noses, and expelling them with disgrace from the town.

The siege commenced about the latter end of *October*. In *November* the regular Infantry of Juggoo Bappoo drove in the Bhopal out-posts, as before mentioned; and in the beginning of *December*, the enemy took up the positions that have been detailed, to blockade the town gates; shortly after this, Vizier Mahomed was informed of a spot where treasure was supposed to be concealed. He ordered the ground to be dug up, and found 22 large bags or sacks, containing each 8 or 10,000 pieces of copper. (78) He also found 30 small iron guns, in good condition: these he directed to be mounted on the walls, while the copper was coined, and distributed to the troops. Grain had now become no scarce, that only two seers (79) were procurable for a rupee. It has been stated, that every road to the town was blocked up by the enemy. But, the town of Bhopal is defended by a large lake on the western side, over which grain was, from time to time, transported in boats, for the use of the besieged, by some of the principal zemindars, or landholders, of the country, and particularly by Ruttun Singh. The progress of the besiegers was slow during the first two months. The wall of the town of Bhopal was high and strong, and the Artillery of the enemy seldom fired more than 40 shots in a day, except on occasions of their making an attack. None had yet been made upon the body of the town; but about the middle of *December*, a general assault took place. A storming party was directed upon every gate, whilst others attempted to escalade

(78) Not above the value of a few thousand rupees were obtained by this search, no treasure was found; only pieces of copper.

(79) A seer is 80 rupees in weight; and, according to the Oujeen rupee, this may be estimated about 2 pounds avoirdupois.

the walls; but they were repulsed at every point; though not till after a conflict which lasted 18 hours. The conduct of Vizier Mahomed on this occasion, gave great courage and confidence to the troops, and to the inhabitants. He flew himself, or sent succour, to every point that was pressed, till attack after attack was abandoned, in despair by the assailants.

1814. In the month of *January* two different assaults on the town were made at the same time—one by Sadick Ali, on the Gunnour gate, and the other by Dan Singh, on the Mungulwarra gate. Some of the assailants were so successful as to effect an entrance by escalade over a part of the wall which had been battered near the top; but they met with so warm a reception from the defenders within, that the whole of them were forced to retreat. The partial success of the attack on the Mungulwarra gate, having attracted the attention of the besieged, who all crowded to that quarter, the defence of the Gunnour gate was neglected; and a party were enabled to escalade the wall, and gain a bastion, where they planted their standard. This display, however, afforded but a short-lived triumph; as the *women* of this quarter of the town, alarmed at the danger which threatened them, assembled in crowds on the tops of houses, and other high places, and attacked the enemy with a shower of tiles, stones, and other missles. The unexpected annoyance from the *Amazons* galled the assailants so severely, that they were compelled to lower their standard, and could hardly maintain their ground. At this juncture, Vizier Mahomed, having repulsed the attack at the Mungulwarra gate, arrived opposite to that at the Gunnour gate, where he was equally successful, forcing those who had entered to retire precipitately and with great loss. Another account states that the scaling ladders were thrown down, which left the assailants without retreat, and that the greater part of them were destroyed.

Vizier Mahomed was quite delighted with the conduct of the *women* who had defended this unguarded post; and after highly applauding their courage, he rewarded them with presents for the essential service which they had performed. No event that occurred, gave Vizier Mahomed such satisfaction as this. He was of a very sanguine temper, and inclined to superstition; and he drew a happy presage, from the display of valor made by the females of the town upon this occasion,—that the place was not destined to fall into the hands of the besiegers. The situation, however, of the defenders of Bhopal, became every day worse: during the month of *February*, the price of the coarsest grain rose to the rate of a rupee per seer, (or two pounds,) while the usual price of the best grain was 20 seers the rupee. The boats had hitherto continued to bring occasional, though scanty supplies; but this mode of relief was discovered by the enemy, who bribed the boatmen to desert. This misfortune reduced the besieged to such distress, that numbers of the inhabitants, as well as the troops, were unable to resist the opportunity which offered of withdrawing; which, with casualties, diminished the number of the garrison from 6,000 to as many hundreds. The Mahomedan part of this body did not scruple to eat carrion; while the most rigid of the Hindoos, endeavoured to appease the cravings of hunger by making food of bruised tamarind-stones, and the leaves of trees. They, however, at times received assistance from the besiegers themselves: some of whom, tempted by exhorbitant profit, furnished, by stealth, supplies of grain, which were handed over the walls.

During this month (*February*) some more efforts were made by Dan Singh, but with such unvaried bad success, that it excited the indignation of another commander, named Ram Lal, who resolved to make a desperate attack, boasting that he would in the course of next day be in possession of the town. In furtherance of this determination, he prepared an assaulting party of 3,000 chosen men, with which he marched before daybreak upon Viziergunj. The troops stationed at this point were fortunately, on the alert, and opened a smart fire which gave the alarm to the besieged in the town the latter immediately sent out two guns to their support, which, with those from the walls; and from Futtygurh, were so well served, and did such execution, by a cross-fire, amongst the enemy, that when day broke, nearly 1,000 of them were killed and wounded. The assailânts notwithstanding this loss, pushed boldly on till they advanced so close to the walls of Bhopal, as to be under cover from the cannon. At this crisis, Vizier Mahomed, with only 50 men, made a sally from the Jumarath gate, and the party of Vizier-gunj sallying from thence at the same time; they made, conjointly, an attack upon the enemy with such desperate resolution and ardour, that they forced them to retreat, with their numbers reduced from 3,000 to little more than 500. Vizier Mahomed lost on this occasion 60 or 70 of his best men, which, with other casualties, lessened his adherents to the small number of 200. But Ram Lal, one of the bravest of the leaders of his enemies, was so much dispirited and affected by the loss of so many men, that he would never venture upon another assault.

Grain was not now procurable in Bhopal, except such as was sold clandestinely by the besiegers; even that was little, and at the enhanced rate of 2 rupees per seer, whilst it continued to be sold in the Mahrattah camp at the rate of one rupee for five seers. To preserve life, the besieged had no other food than that which has been before mentioned, pounded tamarind-stones and *Casnee*; (80) and even these two articles were not to be had under the exhorbitant price of a rupee and a half per seer.

In the month of *March*, the besieged experieñced some respite from hostilities on the part of the enemy, in consequence of the death of Juggoo Bappoo; an event which occupied the Mahrattahs nearly a month. The performance of the funeral obsequies and rites of this chief, appears to have been deemed a duty that superseded every other.

About the end of *April*, one of Vizier Mahomed's officers, named *Doongurh Singh*, who had been stationed with a " party of 100 men (now reduced to 10) to defend the old fort, allowed himself to be tampered with by Sadick Ali Khan; and he not only deserted his post during the night, but conducted about 500 of the enemy into the fort he had abandoned. It chanced that two men stationed at the old fort gate leading to the town, were alarmed at the bustle made by the Nagpoor troops as they entered. They imagined, at first, that it was created by Doongurh Singh returning from his rounds; but, upon attentively listening, they became convinced that

(80) Casnee, or wild succory. It was probably the root of this plant that was used for food.

the noise was that of a larger party than he had under his command. In order to ascertain the fact, they cautiously entered the fort; and on arriving near the Mausoleum of the late Nuwab, Feyz Mahomed Khan, they found it filled by a body of the enemy, with the matches (81) of their fire-arms lighted. On this discovery, one of the men hastened to report the circumstance to Vizier Mahomed, who inquired what had become of *Doongurh Singh;* the other replied that he could not tell, but advised that some prompt and decisive steps should be taken; otherwise the enemy would soon possess the town. On this remark, Vizier Mahomed, who had at that time only 30 men with him, cast as anxious glance at his son, Nuzzur Mahomed Khan, who, construing the expression of his father's eye, into a wish that he should be the first to go against the enemy, entreated permission to do so. "If matters are come to this crisis," said Vizier Mahomed, "we must all go." But, on further solicitation from his son, he permitted him to proceed in advance with 12 men; whilst he, himself, with the remainder of his party followed at a short distance.

1814. In the mean time the enemy had not quitted the Mausoleum, but conceiving themselves already masters of Bhopal, had

(81) The Irregular Infantry of native princes in India use matchlocks.

become neglectful of precaution: many of them had laid their matchlocks aside, whilst others undressing themselves sat down at their ease, enjoying the thoughts of their fancied success. On Nuzzur Mahomed arriving near the Mausoleum, two of the Puthans who were a few paces in advance of the rest, called out, with a view of deceiving the enemy, to those in the rear, "Come on, comrades, the enemy are very inferior to us in numbers." A volley was instantly fired by this small party, which did great execution, as the fire-arms of the Puthans consisted of a kind of blunderbuss, each of which was loaded with 30 or 40 small balls. The enemy were thrown into the greatest disorder and consternation by this unexpected attack. They were also deceived by the call purposely made by the foremost Puthans; and in this state of perplexity were incapable of adopting any plan of defence. Vizier Mahomed with his party joined that of his son, and the whole of this little band of Puthans threw aside their fire-arms, and drawing their swords, rushed with impetuosity into the Mausoleum. Those of the enemy who could escape, offered little or no resistance; but they left behind them above 100 men killed and wounded; and a number of their arms and clothes. Vizier Mahomed was on this occasion most severely bruised with stones, and Nuzzur Mahomed Khan, received a deep sabre-cut on the shoulder, and a slight one on the head. This success was attended with more important consequences than could have been anticipated. In a few days after it occurred (in the beginning of *May*), Sadick Ali Khan, announced his having had a dream, in which he heard a noise uttering awful maledictions against him for his apostacy, in leaguing with infidels against the followers of the most high Prophet. He had been warned, he added, to desist from attempts which were alike futile and impious; for, it was evident that the besieged were under the immediate protection of a Divine Providence (82). The impression, real or pretended, made on Sadick Ali, by this dream, was so great, that he, publicly, declared his resolution of conforming to

(82) In this case, there were two Hindoo Powers (Mahrattahs) attacking a Mahomedan state. Sadick Ali, the Berar Rajah's General, was therefore, fighting against the Faithful, or those of his own religion. According to the *Koran*, this is prohibited. On points of religion (*Deen*) Sheeahs, may fight against Soonnees, supposing one party to act contrary to the well known and acknowledged principles of the Koran At the processions of the Tazeeahs, pains are taken to prevent the two parties (Sheeahs and Soonnees) meeting—They holding different opinions as to the successor of Mahomed In the general affairs of the world, and in domestic matters, there would be no clashing of interests; the general principles of Mahomedanism are the same with both the great divisions of the Faithful; which are, to increase its propagation, therefore, to aid any Hindoo power to crush a Mahomedan state, would by all Mahomedans, be esteemed as acting contrary to the spirit of the Koran. The death of Sindiah's General, Juggoo Bappoo, no doubt, was considered as a prophetic indication of the displeasure of Heaven.

what it dictated, and, in consequence, issued orders to his army to prepare to withdraw from Bhopal. Dan Singh, and others of Sindiah's commanders, used many arguments to induce him to remain; but their intreaties were answered by exhortations to follow his example; if they wished to avoid the vengeance of Heaven.

After the departure of Sadick Ali, which greatly injured the confederate cause, the leaders and troops of Sindiah, fatigued by a harrassing service, which had already lasted nine months, during which they had lost many thousands of their men, without making any substantial progress in their operation, desisted from any further attempts against Bhopal; and, after a fortnight spent in preparation for marching, they raised the siege by moving towards Sarungpoor (83), at which place they contoned. The above is the account given by the late Major General Sir John Malcolm, himself a distinguished officer, and the Hero of Mahidpoor.

Captain James Grant *Duff*, in his history of the Mahrattahs (84) speaks of "the heroism of Vizier Mahomed in the gallant defence of Bhopal." Another authority (85) states that "the

(83) A town in the province of Malwa, on the north side of the river Sopra, 55 miles north-east from Oojeen.

(84) Vol. 3, p. 391

(85) Bengal and Agra Gazetteer, vol. 2, part 2, p 233, A D. 1841.

siege of Bhopal, in 1813-1814, is one of the most remarkable of the time, and the conduct of the chief, whose garrison at the commencement of the siege did not exceed 8 or 10,000 men,—is the theme of praise and admiration of the Mahomedans of India."

The circumstances of this celebrated siege are of so remarkable a nature, that the reader of the military exploits detailed by the various Mahomedan and Hindoo historians, will fail to find the relation of any siege, which so well deserves to be held up to the example and admiration of future ages. It is famed for the skill and talent with which the plan of defence was formed; and for the courage and gallantry with which it was carried into execution.

All accounts are agreed that the enemy's force was very great. Supposing their force to have been 50,000 instead of 70,000 men as stated by some, that of Vizier Mahomed was only 11,000 at the commencement of the operations. But when, owing to want of forage, the 3,000 Pindarries were compelled to leave the town, and the mounted troops belonging to the zemindars had, from the same cause, left the place, Vizier Mahomed's force was reduced to less than 6000 men, (deducting casualties,) of which number nearly half were mounted troops; for the protection of the gates of the town, Vizier-gunj, and the old fort, &c.; the number of Infantry assigned for their defence was only 2,600, with a reserve of 500 men; so that there were only 3,100 infantry. (86) The Cavalry, composing the remainder of the force, were, of course, of little use except as dismounted troops, for there was a want of forage for their horses. When the operations of the siege commenced, the enemy were eight times the number of the besieged. Vizier Mahomed's force was inadequate to the defence of the place, which was four miles in circumference, and though it had a tolerable wall, it had no ditch, or other defence, on three faces; so that were a breach once effected there would be no ditch to cross, and scaling ladders could be easily planted against the walls; or, if a perfect breach, or breaches, were made, the enemy could, by force of numbers, force a passage into the body of the place; and by making several attacks, the force of the besieged, at any one point, would be but small against such overpowering numbers.

	Men.		Men.
(86) The old fort,. ...	100	Vizier-gunj, ...	500
The Gunnour gate	200	Futtygurh............	200
The Gondwarra gate	200	The Bala Killa........	100
The Mungulwarra gate	200	The Sally Port of Futtygurh	100
The Etwarra gate..........	200		
The Jumarath gate	200		2,600
The Sondwarra gate	400	The Reserve...........	500
The Hummamel gate	200	Total	3,100

The fortifications on the heights upon the bank of the Lake, were in a very bad condition, and such imperfect works were rather a weakness to the town: because they would give cover to the enemy, while they could not be defended by a weak garrison. The enemy could receive re-inforcements of troops, while the garrison could not obtain any addition of men; could the garrison have done so, they had not provisions to feed them. In this siege, the bravery of the garrison, and its devoted attachment to its leader, stood in the place of numbers. The justice of a good cause, often sheds round the defenders of the rights and liberties of their country, a halo of protection, which the enemies to good order and peace cannot penetrate. It was the destiny of Bhopal, that there existed in the person of Vizier Mahomed, the saviour of his country.

The arrangements made by Vizier Mahomed for the defence of Bhopal, exhibit, at once, the talent of an able general. He saw that the enemy, confident in their numerical strength, would direct their attacks against the gates of the town; and he accordingly posted parties at each, while he kept a reserve, under his own immediate command, to aid any post requiring assistance. Foreseeing a siege of long duration, for it commenced with the beginning of the cold season, he early warned all the inhabitants to depart who could not assist in the siege. Some with false notions of humanity, view such a measure as harsh and inhuman; but, it is founded upon the wisest principles of Government, that private persons should sacrifice their interests to the public good; and had these people remained, they must have starved both the garrison and themselves; their presence would have tended to cause the fall of the town, and have placed the principality in the hands of its enemies. (87)

In 1812, Juggoo Bappoo, Sindiah's general, had made an attack upon Bhopal and failed, and retired during the rainy season. When the cold season arrived, the troops both of Sindiah and of the Berar Rajah, advanced to make a joint attack. It might be asked, why was not a store of provisions laid in to provide against such an attack? The answer is very easy. In 1806, Islamnuggur had been delivered up to Sindiah, and four lakhs of rupees had been agreed on to be paid, as well as an annual tribute. The pretence for the attack in 1812, was the non-payment of a balance of money due by Bhopal on this

(87) At the siege of Pondicherry in 1760-1761 by Colonel *Coote*, the Governor, *M. Lally*, owing to the want of provisions turned out the native inhabitants, but, even his enemies never questioned the good sense of his conduct on this occasion.—*Mill's* History of India, vol. 3, p. 262.

account. The loss of Islamnuggur and of other possessions, had reduced the resources of the state. Vizier Mahomed found the country, on his return to Bhopal, in a very depressed condition—there did not exist the pecuniary means for the purchase of an adequate supply of provisions. In the disturbed state of Central India, and with the large force of the Mahrattahs in the field; the stored grain in the vicinity of the principality, would be secured by them. The town of Bhopal has many places in which grain can be stored, but, as before the siege money was scarce, so it became more so afterwards; and the garrison could not send out parties to bring in grain, had they possessed money with which to purchase it. There was no wealth in the place; and the inhabitants who left the town, took what little they had with them.

That the garrison would have been starved into a capitulation was certain, had not the Mahrattah grain-merchants,—who accompany armies, and live on the necessities of mankind, and are, indifferent as to the result of the operations, so long as they can gain wealth,—been induced, by the prospect of gain, to send in provisions during the night time, sometimes at a profit of 400 *per cent!* Large quantities could not be supplied without detection, so that the supply, though at a high price, must have been scanty. It may be asked where did the money come from, with which to purchase grain? The grain-merchants must have sold on credit, and have obtained 900 per cent. on their sales of grain: it was not an unsafe speculation, depending for success, on the result of the siege, at a time when the Mahrattahs had failed in their grand attack. It is probable that during the cessation of hostilities consequent on the death of Juggoo Bappoo, a better supply of provisions was obtained by the garrison: without provisions, the perseverance of the garrison would have been useless.

When the garrison were so much reduced in numbers, the defection and treachery of Doongurh Singh was nearly proving fatal to the cause of Bhopal. That an enemy amounting to 500 men should have been driven out of the Mausoleum by 30 men, exhibits one of those feats in warfare, of which there appears to be no parallel. The prompt decision and gallantry of Vizier Mahomed, and of his son, Nuzzur Mahomed Khan, who nobly emulating his father, led the advance of a party to attack sixteen times their numbers; could alone have defeated such a very superior an enemy; of whom they killed three times their own number. Thus, though the treachery of Doongurh Singh placed in jeopardy the town of Bhopal, the occurrence afforded a brilliant opportunity of proving, in addition to former gallant deeds, the unrivalled resolution and gallantry of Vizier Mahomed. It was the crowning act in the defence of Bhopal.

The grand attack made in the middle of December, 1813, commenced, it has been ascertained, about one and a half hour before day-break, so that the attack which lasted 18 hours embraced several hours of darkness; a period very favorable to the large force of the enemy, whose points of attack and numbers, would not be discernible; there being no moon during the *night* of the attack (88). The duration of the attack is very unusual in Indian warfare; and, when it is considered that the garrison were naturally reduced in physical strength from living so long on bad and scanty provisions, by which they were less capable of such a lengthened defence, while the enemy had plenty of food, the defence is the more remarkable. There seems no doubt that the Mahrattahs hoped, by continuing the attack, to wear out the garrison, and that during the darkness of night, they would be unable to prevent an entrance into the town: all these considerations, however, tend to render the defence so much the more memorable; and the result unexpected, according to all the common chances of warfare. In the two subsequent attacks in January, 1814, the enemy, when they had

(88) By the Almanac for 1813, it appears that the last quarter of the moon was on the 14th of December, 1813.

obtained a partial success, by entering a bastion, found, even in the *women* of the town, defenders they little calculated upon; and by whom they were driven from the position they occupied. This event gave courage to all, and exhibited a noble conduct on the part of the females of Bhopal, and well might Vizier Mahomed draw a happy presage of success from such an event. It proved to the enemy, that every man and every woman were determined defenders. It exhibited a high feeling of patriotism and of devotion to the chief, who was considered "the saviour of his country."

The attack on Vizier-gunj outside the town by 3,000 men, which preceded that made by Vizier Mahomed on the Mausoleum, proved the astonishing courage and boldness of the defenders of Bhopal: recollecting that the whole force in Bhopal did not amount to above 200 men; and though in this attack several guns were used by Vizier Mahomed. This attack so discouraged the enemy, that they never ventured to make another assault. It is obvious, supposing the enemy to have lost several thousands of men during the siege, that a blockade must have caused the fall of the town: but, the death of Juggoo Bappoo, and the dream of Sadick Ali, and the several defeats against such an inferior force, caused the enemy to lose courage. Had the enemy succeeded in keeping possession of the old fort, supplies would have been thrown into the town with more difficulty. Thus ended this celebrated and memorable siege, which had lasted nine months, during which the garrison was reduced, after the Pindarries and the troops of the zemindars had been forced to withdraw for want of forage, from 6000 to less than 200 men. Most garrisons would long before the termination of the siege, have surrendered to the enemy, considering it a hopeless case: and, indeed, had not the Mahrattah grain-merchants supplied provisions, it would have been impossible to have held out, even against a tenth of the force employed against the place. (89)

(89) It is related that, at one time during the siege, Vizier Mahomed himself, almost thought it would be impossible to hold out against such an overwhelming force. A *fuqueer*, whether a Mahomedan or Hindoo was never known, had been at Bhopal for 12 years. Vizier Mahomed went to him, and taking off his Turban and sword, placed them at the feet of the *fuqueer*, saying, "I have only so many troops—how can I defend this place against so many thousands, by whom Bhopal is now surrounded." The *fuqueer*, thinking a little, said, "take up your sword and go 'mar' (fight) the scoundrels, and you shall be victorious" Vizier Mahomed took up his turban and sword and returned into the city It has been stated before, that Sadick Ali Khan, the Nagpoor Rajah's general, had a dream. It is not known whether he, or one of his superior officers heard it; but a voice was heard, issuing from a burying ground. The words said to have been uttered were, "*mar, mar, mar,—strike, strike, strike.*" The verb "*marna,*" also means to "conquer."' After the enemy's armies left Bhopal the fuqueer disappeared. Though there had been sentries posted to watch him on his first coming to Bhopal, no one could ever observe him to eat, or to sleep. He went to a mountain where he now is. He is said to be 100 years old, and not to have a white

1814. The danger to the city of Bhopal was not yet over. Juswunt Rao Bhow, the cousin (90) of the late Juggoo Bappoo, who had succeeded to the command of Sindiah's troops, employed himself during the rainy season, in making preparations for renewing the siege the moment the season would permit. Vizier Mahomed, who, though his means and numbers were reduced to the lowest ebb, still preserved an unbroken spirit, employed himself, during the rainy season, in sending grain and stores from Raiseen to Bhopal; to enable him to sustain another attack (91). His difficulties, however, appeared insurmountable; to recruit his troops was not an easy matter; the Pindarries had all joined the camp of the Bhow, and that was now re-inforced by *Jean Baptiste*, a European (92) commander in the service of Sindiah, who brought a well equipped Cumpoo, or brigade, of eight battalions and above 40 guns. Fortunately for Bhopal, a serious dissension now occurred amongst its enemies. The refusal of Juswunt Rao Bhow

hair on his head. He made a prophecy seven years ago, the result of which may be soon known.

(90) Juswunt Rao Bhow, was the son of Jewda Dada, the first cousin of Juggoo Bappoo

(91) The city of Bhopal could contain supplies of grain for any period

(92) Though called a European, he was born in India. He is the half-brother of Colonel Filoze, celebrated for having betrayed Nana Furnavese, the Peshwah's minister. (See Toone's Letter on the Mahrattahs.)

to make an advance of money to pay the troops of Baptiste, was the first ground of discontent: this was daily aggravated, till a chance quarrel between a party of their foragers, caused each to draw out his troops, and a serious affray ensued. But the followers of the Bhow, particularly the Infantry which had suffered extremely during the siege, were not able to stand against the fresh and better disciplined brigades of Baptiste; they fled in every direction, leaving their camp to be plundered. This action took place at Sehore, (93) where Baptiste is said to have taken 103 guns of different sizes. The Bhow and some of the leaders took refuge under the walls of Bhopal, where they were permitted to shelter themselves for one night; but requested to depart early next day as it was apprehended that their remaining there might be a motive for another attack; which, if aided by the renewal of a hostile combination, would probably, have effected the destruction of this principality, in spite of the heroic efforts made in its defence That Baptiste did not prosecute the siege has been variously accounted for, but the real cause was, that the overture made by Vizier Mahomed, at this period, to the British agent in Bundelkund (94) had been so far favorably

(93) Sehore is about 24 to 26 miles from Bhopal

(94) The late Mr. Wauchope, Governor General's agent in Bundelkund.

entertained, that the Resident at the court of Gwalior (95) had called upon Sindiah to abstain from prosecuting hostilities against Bhopal. There was another object besides the protection of Bhopal: that of repressing the Pindarries, whose excesses now menaced the general peace of India. (96) The Resident at Nagpoor (97) also, to whom Vizier Mahomed had sent an agent, evinced equal penetration in the delineation he so early gave of the actual condition and character of the principality of Bhopal, its local advantages, and friendly disposition. This is Sir John Malcolm's statement of the case. It had in 1809, been erroneously supposed, but that rested on the declaration of Sindiah chiefly, that the Nuwab of Bhopal had encouraged, in fact, given an asylum to the Pindarries. Vizier Mahomed satisfied Colonel (afterwards Sir Barry) Close on this point. We have, also, seen that when Juswunt Rao Bhow came to make a second attack on Bhopal, that "the Pindarries had all joined the camp of the Bhow." In 1814,

(95) Mr. Strachey. This Sir John Malcolm confirms, and states that our interference alone prevented Baptiste's attack on Bhopal. The Bengal and Agra Gazetteer states "the Residents at Gwalior and Nagpoor, interposed their mediation in consequence; and the hostile designs of those courts were abandoned" Vol 2, part 2, p. 234.

(96) They commenced their plundering operations in 1812

(97) Mr. (now Sir Richard) Jenkins's Letter to Mr. Secretary Adam, dated 29th October, 1814.

the Residents at the courts of Gwalior and Nagpoor, both pointed out the aid to be derived by a connexion with Bhopal.

In relation to the proposed renewal of the attack on Bhopal, it is of value to adduce the statement of Captain J. G. *Duff*, (98) who, when Resident at the Court of Satara, had the means of knowing what was the nature of the proposed renewal of hostilities by the Mahrattahs against Bhopal. He states that "Lord Hastings obtained information, that a negotiation for a treaty, offensive and defensive, was in progress betwixt Sindiah and Raghojee Bhonslah (the Nagpoor Rajah), and also between Sindiah and the minister of Toolsee Bye Holkar (99). These negotiations were the preclude to the treaty of confederacy, of which the first article, expressed the determination of these princes, to serve and obey the Peshwah. (100) "The Marquess," he further states, "learnt that Sindiah, who had made great efforts against Bhopal the preceding year, was determined to renew the siege; that, in its exhausted state, even the heroism of Vizier Mahomed must prove unavailing; and, finally, that this chief earnestly solicited to be taken under

(98) History of the Mahrattahs, vol 3. p. 391.

(99) Thus forming a triple alliance

(100) This may be considered the ground-work or prelude to the Mahrattah War of 1817-1818, in which the Peshwah made the first hostile attack at Poonah on the 5th November, 1817.

British protection. From these circumstances, Lord *Hastings* determined on adopting the proposed measure, and directed certain terms to be offered, which comprehended the free ingress, egress, and residence of British troops within the Nuwab's territory; and the surrender from Bhopal of a fort as a present depôt. To support these negotiations, the troops in Bundelkund were re-inforced, the Hyderabad subsidiary force moved from Jaulna to Elichpoor, the Poonah subsidiary force from Seroor to Jaffierabad; a large reserve was formed in the Dekhun; and the army of Guzerat occupied a position at Soneepoor, on the bank of the Myhie river. Vizier Mahomed appeared most ready to embrace the terms, and it was in consequence, intimated to Sindiah, by the Resident in his camp, that the principality of Bhopal was under British protection.

In a summary of the administration of the Indian Government from October, 1813, to January, 1823, of the Marquess of Hastings, (101) it is stated that " An agreement was made between Sindiah and the Rajah of Nagpoor, that the forces of both should act under Sindiah, for the reduction of Bhopal The very terms of the agreement betrayed the real object; for Bhopal, when conquered, was to be made over to the Nagpoor Rajah It was obvious that Sindiah only wanted an excuse for bringing

(101) Published by his friends, London, 1824, page 16—19.

the Nagpoor troops into junction with those under his command, in which case he would have found himself at the head of a very powerful army. It was not a moment for hesitation. Had Sindiah's forces, which were assembled and ready to march, once entered Bhopal, shame would have made him risk any extremity, rather than recede upon our intervention. The Nuwab of Bhopal had solicited to be taken under British protection. I was (the Marquess says) at the time on Sindiah's frontiers, with only my escort." At this time our (Bengal) disposable troops were employed against Nepal. "But the case called for decision; and I directed the Resident at Sindiah's court to request that His Highness would forbear any aggression upon Bhopal, as that state had become an ally to our Government. I desired that this communication should be made in the most conciliatory tone; and that the Resident would not report to me the violent language with which it would probably be met by Sindiah, so that there might be no affront to discuss: supposing Sindiah predetermined to go all lengths, any provocation from my message was of no moment. * * * Sindiah, it was, unofficially, reported to me, received the intimation with all the vehemence of language which I had expected. But, notwithstanding his declaration, that he should follow his own course, his troops did not move, and the project against Bhopal was silently abandoned * * * The Resident on a later day made a merit with Sindiah of having suppressed, in his report to me, the offensive tone which he had used ; and His Highness acknowledged the obligation."

Mr. Prinsep states (102) that " At the time of rejecting our alliance, it was discovered, that the Bhoosla was actually engaged in negotiating one of an offensive and defensive character with Sindheea, for the subjugation of the Bhopal principality by their joint arms * * * No sooner was Lord Hastings apprised of these intrigues, than he saw at once the immediate result. * * * He resolved no longer to hesitate in stepping forward to complete his defensive arrangements, by forming a connexion with Bhopal and Sapgur, in despite of any efforts by the regular independent powers to contract the design."

" The Bhopal family had preserved their political independence against the most active efforts of the Mahrattahs in the fulness of their military preponderance; although their position, immediately between the Bhoosla and Sindheea, made their territory the particular object of Mahrattah jealousy, and presented, as long as it should remain inviolate, an effectual

(102) Narrative of the Political and Military Operations of British India, under the administration of the Marquess of Hastings, 1813 to 1818. Quarto, 1820, pp. 36 to 46.

bar to the consolidation of the influence of that nation." As Prinsep well observes, "The importance of saving such a friend, when a hostile combination of the Mahrattahs was to be apprehended, must be obvious enough. (103) Already, in execution of the offensive and defensive engagements between Sindheea and the Bhoosla, was the best appointed force of the former, that commanded by Colonel *Baptiste*, on one part of the frontier; while Sudeek Ulee Khan, with the troops of Nagpoor, approached it on the opposite side; and another division of Sindheea's troops, that under Juswunt Rao Bhâo, was also in the neighbourhood. No time was to be lost Sindheea had before frequently attacked this state, and even besieged its capital, but without success (partly owing to the incapacity of the commanders he employed, and the general ignorance of the mode of attacking fortified places; and partly owing to the gallantry and skill of Vizier Mahomed's defence). The Maha Raja, however, had never before entered Bhopâl with so efficient an army, and *Baptiste's* knowledge of European tactics and long and successful practice in the various sieges he had hitherto conducted, seemed to leave but little hope that Vizier

(103) The Nuwab of Bhopal had assisted in 1778 our army under General *Goddard*, when there was a combination of Mahrattahs against us · so that it was only a proper return for an old act of friendship.

Mahomed would be able to save himself, and his dominions, on this occasion. His perpetual hostility to the Mahrattahs had naturally made him look to us in the hour of extremity; and that hour was fast approaching. He was accordingly induced to make a very earnest solicitation for our support, and for that purpose despatched an agent to Dehlee, who waited on Mr. (now Sir Charles) *Metcalfe*, (104) the British Resident there; and submitted, on behalf of his master, a specific proposition to be admitted within the pale of our protection." The Governor General instructed Mr. Metcalfe "to entertain the proposition, and, in case the agent should be furnished with powers sufficiently ample and explicit, to conclude with him an engagement on the following basis:—'The British Government to afford its protection against the present designs of Sindheea and the Bhoosla, and a perpetual guarantee for the future; and the Nuwab to be left in complete independence in the management of his internal administration;—the British troops to have free ingress and egress through the Bhopal territories, together with every facility in the provision of their supplies and necessaries; a fortress to be delivered as a present

(104) Afterwards Secretary to the Government of India, Member of Council, Lieut.-Governor of Agra, acting Governor General when Lord William Bentinck left India in 1835. Subsequently Governor of Jamaica, and now Governor General of Canada

depôt, and, enventually, a spot to be allotted for a cantonment, or permanent station; the Nuwab to renounce all connexion with the Pindarees, (105) and not to negotiate with other powers, except in concert with the British Government; abiding by its arbitration in all differences with them. However, it was thought proper to hold out the prospect of some advantage by way of inducement to enter into an alliance of this nature—the recovery of all the territories of the state, then in hands of the Pindarees, was to be proposed; and the Governor General prepared himself to abandon the claim of a money consideration for the expense of defending the territory; though the demand of a proportion of the charge, if contested, was not to be hastily relinquished.' As the agent at Delhee had not full powers from the Nuwab of Bhopal, the negotiation was removed to Bundelkhund, which, from its vicinity, seemed to be the most convenient spot for conducting it." Colonel *Doveton*, the commandant of the Nizam's subsidiary force, began his march from Jalna on the 3rd of November, 1814; and it was intended that, with this army, he should penetrate into Bhopal, to execute the protective stipulations of the treaty with the Nuwab Vizier."

(105) The *Pindarries* had themselves gone over to the Bhow when he came with Sindiah's army, a second time, to besiege Bhopal: so that the renunciation on Vizier Mahomed's part was accomplished by their desertion of him!

"The negotiations having been thus opened, Mr. *Wauchope* addressed a letter to the Nuwab of Bhopal, explaining at length, the terms on which the Governor General was disposed to receive that state under protection, in compliance with the solicitations of the agent of his court, preferred at Delhee. He hinted, also, at the Nuwab's bearing some part of the expense. An immediate answer was received from Vizier Mahomed, agreeing to all the stipulations proposed, with exception of the delivery of a fort for a present depôt, and of bearing a part of the expense; (106) for the discussion of these two points, he declared his intention of deputing an envoy, as soon as the return of the person he had sent to Dehlee, who was daily expected. The Resident at Sindheea's court, (107) conceiving the Nuwab of Bhopal's unqualified consent to all the fundamental articles of the Governor General's proposition, to amount to a preliminary adjustment of the terms of alliance, proceeded forthwith to make the official communication to Sindheea, of the intentions of the British Government in respect to Bhopal, on advice of the substance of the Nuwab's reply to Mr. Wauchope. Sindheea, on receiving the communication, inveighed in the

(106) There were treasure and jewels in Nuzzurgurh, which caused the objection; and it is stated that Vizier Mahomed offered to pay 30 lakhs of rupees as his share of the expenses.

(107) Mr Richard Strachey.

strongest terms against our interference with the affairs of Bhopal; declaring the principality to be one of his dependencies in Malwa, with which we were solemnly pledged by treaty to have no concern. The Resident denied that it fell within the terms of the treaty, asserting it to be a free and independent state. Gopal Rao Bhao, who took a prominent part in the discussion, declared the several places which had been wrested from Vizier Mahomed by Sindheea, at different times, to be cessions in lieu of tribute justly due, (108) the account of which was still unsettled; and represented our interference to prevent the enforcement of these, his just dues, as tantamount to a positive declaration of war! In point of fact, according to the Mahrattah notions of political justice, Sindheea had a good title to whatever he could extort from Bhopal; and, having been in the habit of making usurpations, and levying contributions on this territory, as his peculiar and exclusive prey; he, conceived no one else had any right to interpose. It was notorious, however, that Vizier Mahomed had long maintained a most glorious struggle for his independence; and neither had himself, nor had any of the family before him, ever by treaty, or other act of any kind, acknowledged the supremacy of any Mahrattah state."

(108) See the year 1806.

"The discussion on this point grew particularly warm, Sindheea taking an active personal part in them, and using language which might have been construed into menace, and when, at the close of the interview, Mr. *Strachey* requested that Colonel *Baptiste* might be ordered to refrain from active hostility against Bhopal, until the Governor General's instructions upon the resident's report of the conference should arrive; the request was distinctly refused. This conference took place on the 30th November, 1814, and the tone then assumed by the Durbar was no wise lowered at an interview obtained by Mr. Strachey's moonshee three days after. A similar communication was made to the other Mahrattah courts. The Nagpoor Raja required time to consider of his answer; but, on being pressed by Mr. *Jenkins*, privately, assured that gentleman, that Sudeek Ulee Khan should be forbidden to join the army of Baptiste, or to act hostilely against Bhopal. It was further ascertained, that this court would not oppose the advance of the subsidiary force at Ellichpoor, through the portion of its territories which lay on the route from that station to Bhopal, in case events should require its movement in that situation A private correspondence, however, was kept up the whole time, between the Bhoosla and Sindheea; and intrigues, which had before been commenced in other quarters, were carried on with renewed activity. The Peshwah, on being informed of the intentions of the British Government, in respect to Bhopal, professed to be highly satisfied, because of the security that would result to the Jageers of several of his dependants in the neighbourhood Among others, the Vinshore Kur, in whose concerns he took particular interest, had large possessions about Ashta and Shujawulpoor, which the Pindarees and Sindheea's commanders were continually plundering, and of the greatest part of which they had already divested him. Notwithstanding the exterior appearance of amity assumed at Nagpoor and Poona, which, in the case of the former, was carried so far as to produce an offer by Ragoojee of a body of his troops to be taken into British pay, and the pressure of this offer with some importunity; there was still little reason to doubt that both these courts, were heartily bent upon the combination, which accounts from every quarter during the months of November, and December, 1814, and January, 1815, reported to be organized against the British power. At the same time that he, (the Governor General) proffered protection to Bhopal and Sâgur, and made these arrangements in support of that measure, he put four divisions in condition to take the field against the Nipâlese."

1815. Captain *Duff* states, that (109) "Sindiah protested most vehemently against the measure; declared the Nabob to be his depéndant, and in defiance of the assembled armies, threatened an immediate attack upon him. His battalions advanced, and although under a certain assurance, that an attack on Bhopal would occasion an immediate rupture with the English, Sindiah, for a time, seemed quite determined to risk the event; but his actions fell short of his words; and ultimately, his army was withdrawn. (110) His conduct was to be accounted for in the unfavourable commencement, (111) and brilliant termination of the Nepaul war; but the first impression throughout India, respecting that warfare, inspired hopes in all, who wished the overthrow of the British power. Of that number, the Peishwa, *** may be considered the chief; it was, however, at one time supposed, that the plan of the general confederacy already mentioned, did not originate with the Mahrattahs, but was suggested through Sindiah by the Nepaulese." (112) Sir John Malcolm says (113) that Vizier Ma-

(109) Vol 3, p. 392.

(110) This differs from Lord Hastings's account

(111) The failure in the first operations against Kalunga, 31st October, 1814.

(112) Of this there is no doubt, the object being to employ our troops, and prevent a larger force being employed against Nipal!

(113) Page 412.

homed Khan when relieved from the pressure of misfortune, did not pursue his object of obtaining the protection of the English, with the same ardour he at first exhibited, and the negotiations that ensued were never matured into any engagement during his life; yet the knowledge of his being in constant communication with the public officers of the British Government was no slight shield, as it deterred his most powerful enemies from attacking him. (114) Captain *Duff* states, that (115) "As long as he was threatened by Sindiah, he not only appeared to accede to the terms, but gave out that he was under the protection of the British; but when the danger subsided, he objected to the surrender of a fort, and the negotiation terminated. ** The failure of this arrangement, prevented the prosecution of any plan of settlement with Govind Rao, Nana at this period." (116) It does not appear why Vizier

(114) This is an error It required more than any such supposed promise of protection: for even the Marquess's declaration, but just prevented Bhopal being attacked: the obstacle to the conclusion of any fixed engagement, is explained by note 106!

(115) Vol. 3, p. 393.

(116) Govind Rao, the Nana of Jaloun did afterwards; *Prinsep*, p. 229. But Vizier Mahomed was perfectly sincere in his desire to place himself under our protection, ever since he first solicited it in 1805; and in 1809, when Colonel *Close* crossed the Nerbuddah, and the Nagpoor force was in his country, he again pressed it. *Malcolm*, says, p. 395, (1809,) speaking of the rejection of "all his propositions which he then made, and often repeated during the seven years of his arduous and unsupported struggles, to maintain

Mahomed's engagement not being carried into execution, affected Govind Rao, Nana of Jaloun, in Bundelkund. The difference of opinion between Vizier Mahomed and the British Government, was as to giving up the fort (Nuzzur-gurh), which was misunderstood.

1816. Vizier Mahomed was now secure from the attacks of his enemies, but Sir John *Malcolm* says, "He was, nevertheless, continually engaged in that predatory warfare, amid which he had lived, and of which the territories of the state that he governed, had long been the focus. One of the last actions of his life, was an effort to reconcile, by intermarriages, his family with that of Ghous Mahomed. The daughter of Ghous Mahomed (117) was married to Nuzzur Mahomed Khan, the second and favorite son of Vizier Mahomed; while the latter chief gave the eldest son of the Nuwab (Ghous Mahomed) his niece; the daughter of Kurreem Mahomed, the present (118) minister of Bhopal."

1816. Malcolm says, that "Vizier Mahomed died in February, 1816, (119) aged 51 years, after having governed Bhopal little more than

the existence of the state of which he was the head;" confirms his anxiety for protection.

(117) The present Begum mother.

(118) In 1832. His great-grandfather was the elder brother of Dost Mahomed Khan, the founder of Bhopal.

(119) Captain Duff says, "he died on the 17th of March, 1816, and Rughoojee Bhonslay on the 22nd of March, 1816.

nine years: but of this short period he had not passed one day in repose. This principality, from the hour he assumed the government until the hour of his death, was threatened with destruction. Such a man could alone have saved it. Though as remarkable for prowess and valor as the most distinguished of the Affghan race, he was, in his manners, mild, and pleasing; but his look and stature were alike commanding, and there was in his disposition a sternness and determination of purpose 'that inspired awe.'" He is said by Major *Henley* (120) to have died of an inflammatory fever, after a short illness of four days. All acquainted, as Sir *J. Malcolm* observes, "with the vicissitudes of his life, deeply regretted his death at the moment it occurred. He should have lived to behold his patriotic efforts rewarded; to see the people of the land he loved rescued from destruction, and raised to happiness and prosperity by the Government which he had through life courted, and on which his hopes till the last hour of his life rested. (121) This destiny was reserved for a son whom he selected and educated as his successor, and who proved himself every way worthy of his father." Only a year before his death, Vizier Mahomed found himself deserted

(120) Who was the Political Agent at Bhopal about two years afterwards.

(121) By the British Government under Lord *Hastings*.

even by the Pindarries, whom he, in his extremity, had called on for assistance; this was the period when Juswunt Rao Bhow and Baptiste, Sindiah's generals, were about to besiege Bhopal a second time; which danger, had it not been averted, the fall of that principality was certain. Sindiah, the Nagpoor Rajah, the Peshwah, Holkar, Ameer Khan, and the Pindarries, were all leagued against him. Any unfavorable termination of the war in Nipal in 1815, would have caused his destruction; for the confederacy would have joined to a man; and Vizier Mahomed, in an endeavour to save the state, must have placed himself under the protection of Sindiah; so that he would not have lived to have witnessed the glorious result of his great efforts, in his country's cause. Such indeed would have been a result to be deplored; as the destruction of the Bhopal principality, would have proved fatal to Central India: and the British Government must, with regret, have witnessed the fall of its best friend. But, the destiny of Bhopal was in the ascendant.

1816. Nuzzur Mahomed Khan, who has been so conspicuously mentioned, as the leader of the advance of the small party which attacked, and drove out the enemy from the old fort in the year 1814, which, while it established his fame and reputation as a soldier; was the crowning deed of gallantry, by which Bhopal was relieved from its enemies. This Nuzzur Mahomed Khan succeeded his noble father, as Nuwab, when about 25 years of age. (122) Vizier Mahomed had early determined upon his successor, whose education was an object of his earnest solicitude; and, in addition to all his other acquirements, Nuzzur Mahomed had learnt so well the duties of a soldier, that on his father's death, he stood the first in fame among the chiefs of the country. The respect for the memory of his father, combined with his own high qualities, made all the nobles press the government of Bhopal upon his acceptance." (123) *Prinsep* says, (124) "Vizier Mahomed was succeeded by his son Nuzzur Mahomed, a very young man, too

(122) Captain *Duff*, vol. 3 p. 393, says, "Wuzeer Mahomed was succeeded, as Nabab of Bhopal by his son *Wuzeer Mahomed* and Rughoojee Bhonslay (Nagpoor) by his only son Pursajee." But Malcolm is known to be correct. The eldest son of Vizier Mahomed was *Ameer Mahomed Khan*, but not a full brother of Nuzzur Mahomed: he had, however, a son named *Wuzeer Mahomed*. Owing to the idiotism of Pursajie, his cousin, Moodajee (usually styled *Appa Sahib*, whose conduct and escape while a prisoner under the escort of Captain Brown, in 1818, is so well known) was chosen Regent. "Pursajee Bhoosla," *Prinsep* says, "before his accession was known by the name of *Bala Saheb*."

(123) *Malcolm* says, "Ghous Mahomed, who, though he lived a retired life, was still called Nuwab, made no objection to the elevation of Nuzzur Mahomed Khan, and his elder brother, Ameer Mahomed Khan, who also lived in retirement, was among the first to avow, publicly, his own disqualification, and to urge his younger brother to take upon himself the administration of the affairs of the state. To this Nuzzur Mahomed consented."

(124) Page 112.

young it was to be feared, for the perilous circumstances of the principality, superadded to the troubles of a new succession. There was every reason, therefore, to apprehend, that either the Mahrattahs or the Pindaree chieftains in the neighbourhood, would attempt to avail themselves of the occasion, and to interfere in the concerns of Bhopal, in either of which cases, a second and more sincere application of our permanent protection of its legitimate prince, was to be expected as a natural consequence. The question, whether or no the Supreme Government should now direct its efforts to the accomplishment of these two objects (125), was thus forced upon the consideration of the Governor General in Council, in the month of April, 1816." * * * It was now recommended, not only as a measure ancillary to the Nagpoor alliance, but also as a means of gaining a vantage ground for striking a blow at the predatory associations, which the Supreme Government was still left free to inflict, should any opportunity offer of catching their bands beyond their proper boundaries. The objections urged against forming such a connexion, had their foundation, apparently, in the apprehension of the risk of giving umbrage to the Mahrattah powers, which the steps taken in 1814 and 1815 had

(125) With regard to Nagpoor and Bhopal · to establish a subsidiary force at the former

proved to be an object of exaggerated alarm. (126)

1817 Prinsep says, (127) "In the beginning of January, 1817, an agent of the Nuwab, named *Inayet Museeh,* went over to Nagpoor, and there delivered a specific proposition, in writing, to Mr. Jenkins, the Resident, soliciting on the part of Nuzzur Mahomed, that the state might be admitted to British protection, on the terms offered to Vizier Mahomed. This was followed up by a letter to the same effect, from the Nuwab himself to Mr. *Wauchope,* the Political Agent in Bundelkund. Sir J. *Malcolm* says that "the first step of the Campaign of 1817 (against the Pindarees (128), was an

(126) Malcolm says, p 415, "Nuzzer Mahomed's first efforts were directed to the favorite object of his father's life, a treaty of Peace" (*Alliance*) "with the English Government. The policy of this measure had long been under discussion, and a fear of the embarrassment it might produce, had led the Indian Government in *England,* to desire that no such treaty should be concluded; but the outrages committed by the Pindarees forced the Governor General to a course of measures which made obedience to such restrictive orders impossible" The Government in England was not fully acquainted with the state of affairs in Central India, and appear to have supposed that the Pindarries might be easily put down without any ulterior measures. They were unaware of the fact, that the Pindarries were auxiliaries to Sindiah, the Berar Rajah, Holkar, and Ameer Khan, &c , that these powers would, willingly, allow them to go forth and plunder our provinces (as they had done Ganjam in 1812), unsettle the country, and then, declare they had no control over these plunderers!

(127) Page 125.

(128) Commenced in October, 1817. But Lord Hastings had ample proof in 1816, that he was not alone to prepare to act

engagement with the state of Bhopal, concluded at Hussingabad (129), which guaranteed that territory to its actual ruler, and stipulated for his aiding the British army with a contingent, and co-operating to the utmost of his means in the ensuing War." The Nuwab was to "furnish a contingent of 600 horse and 400 infantry for the service of the British Government when required, and when necessary the whole disposable forces were to join the British army." (130) No obligations were ever more faithfully fulfilled. Nuzzur Mahomed received, as the reward of his zeal and efforts, the fine province named Punj-Mahal,

against the Pindarries, but to contend against the high native Powers. *Prinsep* says, p. 225, note (*); "A full size impression of Sindheea's seal happened to drop from the turban of one of his emissaries, while in the act of crossing the Ganges at Bithoor. On searching these letters, written with the design of stirring up the *Goorkhas* to make common cause with the rest of the independent powers of India, were found neatly pasted between the leaves of a Sanscrit book of the Vedas, which one of them, travelling as a student, was carrying with him Several sealed and some open letters from the chief himself were found upon them, the former were sent by his lordship to be presented to his highness in full Durbar, unopened and without comment; in order that he might not suppose us to be ignorant of the intrigues and machinations a foot." Sindiah was given to understand that the Marquess was acquainted with the contents of the letter to the Rajah of Nipal.

(129) He states that it was negotiated by himself in concert with Lieut.-Colonel (the late Major General Sir John, G. C. B) Adams, C B. commanding the force there. The Bengal and Agra Gazetteer says the treaty was concluded on the 26th *February*, 1818. It was the 26th of *January*, 1818.

(130) Gazetteer.

or the five districts,'(131) which were taken from a Jahgeerdar (the Vinshore chief) of the Peshwah, and which not only joined the territories of Bhopal, but had formerly been an integral portion of that principality (131). The restoration of the fort of Islamnuggur, subsequently obtained from Sindiah, though of little value, was esteemed beyond all other favors by the ruling family of Bhopal. It contained the tomb of the Nuwab Yar Mahomed, the son and immediate successor of Dost Mahomed Khan, the founder of the principality; who made it his capital 100 years before the period now referred to; its position, almost at the gates of the capital, had made its separation from the state a source of the greatest annoyance.

1818 The Marquess of *Hastings*, (132) than whom no Governor General knew better how to appreciate the value of the services of the true allies of the British Government, has thus recorded his sentiments. " It was highly gratifying to me, that in this mode (133) I was enabled to bestow on the Nuwab of Bhopal, a splendid reward for the liberality with which he sold all his jewels to maintain troops in aid of our exertions. The fortress and territory of Islamnuggur had been the original posses-

(131) Is said to contain 867 villages Malcolm says, the districts were, Raiseen, Ashta, Sehore, Duraha, and Itchamur.

(132) Summary of his administration p 54 A D. 1824

(133) Territorial arrangements after the Mahrattah War of 1817-18.

sion of his family. In the life time of his father, Sindiah's predecessor had obtained it, through the treachery of the officer to whom it was entrusted; (134) and the strength of the fortress rendered hopeless any endeavour to regain it by siege. This possession, widely separated from the territories of Gwalior, we acquired from Sindiah, by giving him, in exchange, districts greatly superior in value, as well as adjoining his own dominions; and then we conferred it on the Nuwab of Bhopal, as a free gift to recompense his gallant manifestation of gratitude for the protection his country had received in the crisis of the Nepaul War. The Honourable Company will, no doubt, approve the policy of such an exhibited proof, that attachment to their Government was an advantageous course. (135) It must,

(134) The Marquess is in error, he must mean Hoshungabad. Islamnuggur was surrendered to Sindiah in 1806.

(135) The Marquess had previously recorded his opinion of the conduct of the Nuwab of Bhopal "in order to bring the subject" (of the treaty) "to the special notice of the authorities in England." "Nuzurgurh," *Prinsep* says, (p. 219,) "was named as the fort to be required of him for a Depôt Colonel Adams was to advance through the Bhopal territories. Sir T. Hislop and Sir J. Malcolm were to settle the details of the treaty, they were soon expected to arrive on the Nerbudda The Marquess declared to the Council of Fort William, his reasons for deviating from the more limited views that seemed to be entertained in *England*, and expressed a confident hope, that the enlarged plan he had laid down, for the secure and permanent attainment of his object, would meet with the assent of the most considerable princes of Central India. It was his boast," he said, "to have an earnest desire to accom-

here, be remarked, that *Nuzzur Mahomed* sold jewels to aid the cause of peace, to the value of fifty-one (51) or more lakhs of Rupees; upon the sale of which he lost twelve (12) lakhs of Rupees! we may search the history of British India, in vain, to find any similar liberality on the part of any other native state. From the conduct of the reigning Nuwab towards General *Goddard* in 1778, this subsequent exhibition of generosity towards the British Government, "towards which" the agent had declared in 1809, "no extreme of distress could ever make them place themselves in the relation of enemies," was nobly supporting the character of the state, which it has ever since maintained.

Prinsep says, (136) "next to Holkar, the most considerable military chief, under the

plish everything by pacific means, and to be able to declare, with sincerity, that the exclusive object of his present preparations was to get rid of the greatest pest that society ever experienced (the *Pindarries*). He did not hesitate to take upon himself the individual responsibility of acting without the full sanction of the Home Authorities, for he felt confident the result would justify his determination in the eyes of those authorities, and of the British nation at large." *Prinsep* says, p. 427 "The Nuwab signed a preliminary engagement in November, 1817, before the British troops crossed the Nerbudda" *Prinsep*, p. 125, note (*). It is stated in the Bengal and Agra Gazetteer, 1842, vol. 2, part 2, p 367, that his Lordship obtained for Nuwab Asud Ulee Khan, the maternal uncle of the Nuwab of Bhopal, whose minister he was in 1842, the Jagheir of Basoda, which had been siezed by Sindiah, who restored it at the request of the Marquess. He pays no tribute to Sindiah, and wishes to be regarded as a dependant of the British Government.

(136) Page 427.

late settlement, is the Nuwab of Bhopal." * * * As a reward for the cordiality displayed by the Nuwab, the Punj-Muhal, along with some other lands, a part of the Vinshore Kur's fortified Jahgeer, were annexed to Bhopal, whose boundary was by this addition advanced westward as far as the Kalee Sindh. A part of Shujawulpoor was subsequently added, and Islamnuggur was obtained from Sindhiah by treaty. The principality was thus placed on a most respectable footing. The definitive engagement which permanently fixed the relations of the Nuwab, was concluded at Bhopal on the 26th of January, 1818, and ratified by the Governor General on the 8th of March following. The contingent he stipulates to furnish is limited to 600 horse and 400 foot; a low proportion in reference to the resources of the state; but so fixed, expressly to favor the Nuwab. As a more substantial mark of consideration, the obligation of paying tribute, in return for the protection we have engaged to afford, is waved in this instance; notwithstanding that the eventual payment of 125,000 Rupees on this account, was an item of the preliminary agreement, concluded with Lieut.-Colonel Adams and Sir J. Malcolm in November, 1817. Besides, the entire occupation of the Sagur territory, has rendered it expedient to station the military force, required to awe this neighbourhood, within the frontiers of that province; by which arrangement Nuzzur Mahomed is relieved from the obligation of furnishing a cantonment, and surrendering a fort to be converted into a depôt for a stationary British force within his territory, which had also been a part of his original contract.

In closing the war as regards the Pindarries, *Prinsep* says, (137) " such was the extremity of their distress, that Colonel *Adams*, judging them to be now ripe for unqualified submission, caused an intimation to be conveyed to them through the Nuwab of Bhopal, that, if they were willing to throw themselves entirely on the mercy of the British Government, surrendering their arms and horses, the Sirdars might expect a livelihood in some part of our provinces remote from their old haunts, and the lives of their followers would be spared. *Namdar Khan* (138) was the first to avail himself of this information. He delivered himself up to Colonel Adams on the 3rd of February at Deorajpoor in the Bhopal territory, with all his yet remaining followers, which were no more than 87. He required no other terms than a bare assurance that he should not be sent to Europe, or to *Calcutta*. * * * The rest, for the most part, followed the example of Namdar Khan. * * * Thus were the two Dur-

(137) Page 307.

(138) Namdar Khan, it will be recollected, assisted, in 1813, to defend Bhopal.

rahs of *Kurreem Khan* (139) and *Wasil Mahomed,* annihilated. Some were located at Gorukpoor, Ghazeepoor, &c. &c. With regard to Cheetoo, he had wandered about Malwa a short time with about 200 followers; and seeing his affairs to be nearly desperate, endeavoured, through the Nuwab of Bhopal, to make terms for himself, in conjunction with his remaining adherents. For this purpose, he suddenly entered the Nuwab's camp; but when he learned that Nuzzur Mahomed had nothing to offer, beyond a slender personal maintenance in some distant part of *Hindostan,* while he demanded a Jahgeer in *Malwa,* and the entertainment of himself and his men in the British service; he decamped as suddenly as he had come; while he staid, his horses were constantly saddled, and the men slept with the bridles in their hands, ready to fly, instantly, in case of an attempt to seize them. Preparations were making for the purpose the very night he went off; but he was too much on his guard, and too much alive to suspicion, to allow them to be completed. He was instantly pursued by the Nuwab's people, and General Malcolm also sent out parties, to take him, which distressed him so much, that Rajun left him, and made his submission. Mahomed Punah, his son, was likewise made prisoner. Cheetoo found his way to Kandesh and the

(139) Nephew of Namdar Khan

Dukhun, and joined the Arabs and chiefs of the Peshwah's routed army, occasionally protected by the Killadar of Aseergurh. The fate of Cheetoo is well known, he was found dead in the Mahadeo hills, having been killed by a Tiger. Thus, the obstinacy of this Pindarah sealed his fate. The object of locating these people in our own provinces was to induce them to return to the habits of civil life. The *Bheels,* a far more wild tribe, who inhabited the hills in Malwa, &c., were offered by Captain (late Lieutenant Colonel) *Tod,* the Political Agent at Oodeepoor, at the court of the Rana, (the most ancient of the Rhatore Rajpoots) (140) three rupees a month each, if they would cultivate their lands, but he found great difficulty, at first, in inducing these wild people to become civilized human beings; but at length succeeded. (141) Thus, it will be perceived, that Nuzzur Mahomed Khan was the means, in a great degree, of causing the Pindarries to come into terms; that they came in through his means,

(140) This Rana, the head of the Rhatore Rajpoots, is the only Prince who never yielded to the demand of the Emperor of Delhi, for a daughter in marriage, or to occupy a place in the Haram.

(141) The *Bheels* said their fathers and ancestors had never tilled the ground, and why should they They were offered three rupees a month if they would cultivate their lands In a few years they were reclaimed. Sir J *Malcolm,* in 1819, formed a Bheel corps at Mundleysir, and by making the principal chief responsible for his tribe, keep down the plunderers. Those who travelled among their hills, had only to give a present to a chief, who, on giving an *arrow* to the traveller, insured protection on its production, which *force* would not have affected.

since he was the medium of communication: and while he had cause to be displeased with their desertion of his cause in 1814: he, for the general good, forgot their misconduct in his desire to aid the British Government

1818. Never were prospects more flattering than those of Nuzzur Mahomed Khan, (142) when an unhappy accident terminated his life, and left his family and country to mourn the untimely and irreparable loss of a prince, who seemed born for the times in which he lived, and who promised to be as active and successful in restoring his country to prosperity, as his father had been in saving it from destruction. His death was occasioned by the discharge of a pistol he carried about his person, which he laid down when playing in his inner apartment with his infant daughter: (143) and it is supposed to have been fired by his brother-in-law Foujdar Khan, (144) a

(142) *Malcolm*, p. 417. He says, p. 416. "The condition of the Bhopal principality at Vizier Mahomed's death was so low, that its actual revenue could not have amounted to *one lakh* of rupees. It was now rising into importance Its rescued territories included almost all the provinces its princes formerly possessed; and its revenues were improving." Sir John must mean the *town* of Bhopal, and not the principality The principality had still Hoshungabad, Jubbulpoor, Nursingpoor, Hindia, or Baitool

(143) The present reigning Begum of Bhopal called by the family "Secunder Begum."

(144) Son of Ghous Mahomed, consequently uncle to the present Begum, and brother of the Begum mother.

child of eight years of age, who was the only one present on this melancholy occasion. The sensation caused by his death was great, and men gave way to the worst suspicions : but all doubt was soon dispelled, and every suspicion vanished of Nuzzur Mahomed Khan's death being premeditated. It was purely accidental. The child always appeared very fond of the Nuwab. Nuzzur Mahomed was much attached to the Begum, who was then only 17 years of age, and whom he treated with unusual consideration. He not only resisted all the entreaties that were used to induce him to contract a second marriage, (145) but strictly prohibited the introduction of any young females, either as slaves, servants or otherwise, within the Mahal, or palace. The grief of the Begum since the accident was so great, as to produce her miscarriage. There was but one sentiment, that of the deepest regret, and no person sought to take advantage of the accident to promote his own interests. At a consultation of the principal chiefs, it was resolved to continue to attend to the widow and ministers of the deceased prince, till the pleasure of the

(145) That is to marry a second wife Mahomedans are allowed, by the Koran, to have four wives ; but it is considered an honorable exception to the rule, to have only one wife It was a proof of affection in the Nuwab to have only one wife , no doubt, some evil disposed persons wished to introduce some other wife, to divide the Nuwab's affection ; and this from political reasons most probably.

British Government was known as to his successor; (146) and it is remarkable, that not the slightest effort was made by any party to influence the judgment of the British agent; a sufficient proof, of itself, of the absence of all design or guilt on this unhappy occasion.

Nuzzur Mahomed Khan, when he died, was only 28 years of age; he had governed Bhopal, Malcolm says, three years and five months;(147) but he has left a name that has been attained by few during the longest life. Schooled in adversity, he early attained a remarkable maturity of judgment. His appearance was noble, and his manners those of a prince who knew the value of possessing the hearts of his subjects His mind was so superior, and his courage so elevated him above suspicion, that the whole family of the rulers of Bhopal whom he had supplanted, as well as his elder brother who had resigned his birthright to him, lived not only without restriction, but on the most intimate footing of familiarity with him, coming and going through every apartment of his palace at their pleasure. Nuzzur Mahomed held in just detestation the vices and indulgences to which some Mahomedans

(146) Even when there is no doubt as to the succession, it is customary to await the orders of Government regarding the succession.

(147) He succeeded his father in February, 1816, and died in the rainy season (about July) of 1818, so that the period was only 2 years and 5 months

are addicted. His Haram contained but one princess, and no slaves. He was a good Mahomedan, but so far removed from begotry, that his favorite companion and minister, was a *Christian,* by name Shahzad Musseah (148) or Belthazar Bourboun, with whom Sir John *Malcolm* was well acquainted. This person was an able man and a brave soldier, the descendant of a Frenchman, called Bourboun, who came to India in the time of the Emperor Akbar, in whose service he was. (149)

Nuzzur Mahomed's whole soul was absorbed, during the two last years of his life, in plans for improving his country He investigated every account himself, heard every complaint; and, while all speak of his kindness, benevolence and justice, his memory is unstained by the reproach of a single act of tyranny. Sir John *Malcolm* says: " I had, during two years, much communication with Nuzzur Mahomed, and personally knew him; but I rely for the facts above stated, on Major *Henley*, the Political Agent at Bhopal, who enjoyed the fullest opportunities of observing and

(148) He was the son of the agent before mentioned

(149) His father *Enayet Musseah* (Shoohur Bourboun) was born at Gwalior He was the person sent as Agent by the Nuwab (Vizier Mahomed) in 1805, to the Resident in Sindiah's camp. He appears to have possessed a village near Gwalior, which he lost after the Mahrattahs repossessed Gwalior, after its capture in 1780, by Major *Popham*, and to have gone to Bhopal about 60 years ago.

appreciating the character of this remarkable young prince" A greater loss could not have occurred to a community in the condition of Bhopal, than the death of Nuzzur Mahomed Khan; and that event was also a serious misfortune to the British Government, to which this virtuous prince was firmly attached. He was eminently qualified to be the popular instrument which was required to restore order and prosperity. His mind was elevated far beyond the usual range of native Princes. He cultivated knowledge of every description with extraodinary ardour, and had made considerable progress in the arts foreign to the occupations of his life, and the habits of his station. As a proof, it is stated that Nuzzur Mahomed was particularly fond of mechanics; and could himself take to pieces and put together a watch, with the principles of the construction of which he was well acquainted.

Sir John *Malcolm* thus concludes his estimate and eulogium of his character:—"The fame of Nuzzur Mahomed will be long commemorated as an object of emulation to his successors; but we must despair of seeing his equal. He was, as most other such characters have been, formed by the early scenes of his life: (150) no instructions could have conveyed the lessons

(150) When his father began to rule, Nuzzur Mahomed was only 16 years of age, and during the period of warfare, which

he had learnt, when encouraged by the example, and rewarded by the love of a noble father, he struggled with him to preserve a country rendered dearer from the extreme misery to which it was reduced; and his mind was too well formed before the hour of success arrived, ever to lose that tone which it had received amid scenes of difficulty and danger." This is the language of the late Sir John *Malcolm*, who, when he penned this eulogium had 50 years' experience of Indian affairs; had been for 35 years a political officer of the Government; who knew the history of every native state, and the character of every prince in India; who was, himself, a distinguished officer, the Hero of Mahidpoor, in 1819; and who, lastly, held the high office of Governor of Bombay.

Nuzzur Mahomed left no issue by his princess, the daughter of Ghous Mahomed, except one daughter, the present Begum of Bhopal. He had not assumed the title of Nuwab, probably with modest deference to Ghous Mahomed, though he was always addressed as such by the British Government; for Ghous Mahomed, who had long lived in retirement, was never in any way, brought forward in any connexion between Bhopal and the British Government. In the en-

lasted for nine years, he must have had little time to devote to improvement.

gagement which was entered into at Hoshungabad, and in the treaty made after the war, by which the cession to this state, and the amount of the contingent to be maintained, were finally settled, Nuzzur Mahomed Khan and his descendants were alone mentioned; and to them the government of the country was guaranteed. The right of Ghous Mahomed was never agitated. He was *titular* Nuwab, but not *ruler*. Ameer Mahomed, the brother of the deceased, had publicly resigned his birthright, and declared his incompetency; but this abdication of right was very properly, Sir John Malcolm observes, not considered to affect the claims of his children. Mooneer Mahomed Khan, was to have succeeded his uncle, Vizier Mahomed, to whose daughter he was to have been married, that the interests of the family might, as much as possible, have been united in his person. But this marriage never took place, and his younger brother, Jehangier Mahomed Khan, was subsequently married to Secunder, the reigning Begum of Bhopal. It is to be remarked that the obligations and engagements of the British Government have been exclusively contracted with the family of Vizier Mahomed Khan, who alone, have been recognized as rulers of Bhopal.

With regard to the right of succession, Sir John *Malcolm* observes that, "no reference was made to Ghous Mahomed, or to his sons, who are living on the estate assigned for their support at Bhopal; nor do they appear ever to have urged their pretensions. It is, however, worthy of remark, that although the representative of the family of Vizier Mahomed may now be deemed entitled to the name, as well as power of Nuwab of Bhopal, that title was still given by the inhabitants to Ghous Mahomed

The *Murajee Kheil* Puthans of Bhopal, have some singular institutions, which arose out of their original agreement to maintain the habits and laws of their society, such as they existed in Affghanistan. It is from this patriarchal form of Government, that they claim a limited privilege in the selection of their chief; to whom, however, they deny the right of interfering in the jurisdiction of their respective families. The rights of Affghans and other tribes, in this particular, are invariably limited by usage. They must choose a member of the ruling family; and the Murajee Kheil chiefs of Bhopal, appear to have always adhered as closely to hereditary succession, as attention to the general safety, during a state of anarchy and continual warfare would admit. Sir John concludes with these words, so emphatically expressive of the feelings of the chiefs and people :—" *The habits and character of this body of men demand our attention. With every good disposition to the British Government, and gratitude for the benefits they have derived from it, they are not only jealous of encroachment on their usages, but impatient of neglect, and turbulent in a degree that requires much care in conducting our relations with them. They are, however, deserving both of that solicitude and favor which they have hitherto received; for Bhopal is at this moment,* (151) *and will continue while well managed, an essential point of strength in Central India."*

1819. "By an arrangement framed in 1819, (152) by the Begum and the chiefs, and formally recognized by the British Government, Mooneer Mahomed Khan, the nephew of Vizier Mahomed, was declared the successor of the late Nuwab, and betrothed to his only daughter. The regency continued in the hands of the Begum mother, during the minority. But the Nuwab finally relinquished his claim to the hand of the princess, with that of his succession to the throne, in favor of his younger brother." The Begum mother was, at this period, not above 18 or 19 years of age, but she had been well educated; she was able to read and write the Arabic and Persian languages, and possessed such a very superior mind, that she was able, some years afterwards,

(151) 1832.

(152) Bengal and Agra Guide and Gazetteer, 1841, vol. 2, part 2, p 235.

to carry on the affairs of the principality, owing to her extraordinary ability, and aptitude for transacting all state affairs.

1820. "In 1820, (153) the military force of Bhopal, it is stated, consisted of 2,000 cavalry and 5,000 infantry, of which 1,000 were Affghans, from Cabool and Peshawur. The ordnance, garrison and field, amounted to 180 pieces. The revenues were, by the Political Agent, estimated at only nine lakhs of rupees; but, the full revenue, including Jaghiers, under good management, was supposed to be 40 lakhs of rupees." (154).

1824. "In 1824 (155) the important object was attained of organizing the Bhopal contingent, by placing it under the command of a European officer, with whom the distribution of its regular monthly pay, and the promotion of its several ranks, were to rest; to insure such a discipline as would render it available for operations with our forces, and secure its fidelity to the British Government."

1828. "Hakeem Shazad Musseeh, (156) who retired from the office of Dewan, to his Jaghier at Itchawur, died on the 1st of January, 1828. He held for many years the extraordinary position of a *Christian* being the minister of a state like that of Bhopal. In his youth, he was the

(153) Ditto, p. 234

(154) This estimate is very erroneous. The number of guns is far beyond the actual number.

(155) Gazetteer, p. 235.

(156) Ditto, p. 235

friend of the distinguished ruler of Bhopal, Nuzzur Mahomed Khan, became his companion in arms, and distinguished himself as an enterprizing and brave leader; when virtually at the head of the administration, he displayed more rectitude of intention and firmness of conduct in his public capacity, and more integrity and disinterestedness in what regarded his private fortune, than can be often found united in the same individual. Such qualities commanded the respect and confidence of the court, and combined with the expenditure of a large portion of his private income, in unostentatious acts of charity and munificence; secured for him the affections of the people. The general knowledge of the Hakeem, was superior to that of most native princes or gentlemen; while the candid and unreserved manner in which he expressed himself on all subjects, rendered his conversation pleasing. He was succeeded, as minister, by Meean Kurreem Mahomed Khan, who continued satisfactorily to conduct the administration, aided by his Deputy Dewan, Khooshwukt Rae. The Ex-Nuwab, Mooneer Mahomed Khan, who had received on his supercession, a Jaghier valued at 40,000 rupees, (157) guaranteed by the British Government; appeared reconciled to the arrangement regarding himself."

(157) The Begum mother, most generously, gave him, herself, a much larger Jaghier.

1833. Lord William *Bentinck,* Governor General, arrived at Saugor, in January, 1833 (158) The Begum mother, or Regent, as well as other chiefs of Malwa, sent a deputation to meet his Lordship. The Bhopal mission consisted of the Nuwab, (who was accompanied by both his parents,) the minister (Meean Kurreem Mahomed Khan), and all the chiefs of the state. The young Nuwab, after the interchange of the usual ceremonial visits, in a private visit, begged to be placed in immediate possession of power. The Governor General, though much pleased with the intelligence he displayed generally, (159) did not deem that request could then be complied with; but encouraging assurances were given him; on this occasion his Lordship presented two guns to the Nuwab. The Nuwab's parents, on the return of the Mission to Bhopal, retired to Raiseen, and the ex-Nuwab (Mooneer Mahomed) quitted the Nuwab's residence, and retired to a house provided for him in another part of the city. The minister's son (Sidk Mahomed Khan) was at this time appointed Bukshee, or Pay-master. The old minister (Meean Kurreem Mahomed Khan) died in July, 1833, and his son (Sidk Mahomed Khan) received the khillut of investiture as his temporary

(158) Gazetteer, p. 236.

(159) Said to be accomplished, and to well understand Arabic, Persian, and English.

successor: but the Begum Regent shortly afterwards dismissed him from office He had exercised a control over the Begum ; and never allowed her to adopt any course deemed by him objectionable. The Begum, who was about 32 years of age, now determined to look after her own interests. She began to transact business in public, (160) Khooshwukt Rae was appointed temporary minister, and received the khillut and sword of office from the Nuwab's hands; and the title of Rajah Bahadur." The Begum was distinguished by an abhorrence of debt, to discharge which she was ever ready to dispose of her jewels, and make other personal sacrifices; she was liberal to her troops and friends, and a severe judge of such of her servants as were convicted of a breach of faith, or oppression to her poorer subjects. In the choice of her servants charged with the departments of justice and revenue, she showed singular discernment; and, indeed, it was their worth and character which chiefly upheld her and her cause.

On the death of Meean Kurreem Mahomed Khan, *Baboo Seetaram,* a Kunoujeeah Bramin, became Deewan. He had previously been Vakeel at Indore. He was the Deewan of Bhopal about three and a half years, and was succeeded by Khooshwukt Rae. This person went to England in the year 1825, and

(160) Bengum Sumroo did so.

returned to India about two years before Lord William Bentinck came to India, 1828, as Governor General. He again went to England about the end of 1828, with the celebrated Ram Mohun Rae, whose cousin he was. He remained in England about three years, and returned in the same ship with *Bishop Wilson*, the present metropolitan of British India. Ram Mohun Rae died in England in the year 1832.

The state of affairs, in Bhopal, while Seetaram Baboo was Deewan, continued to prosper under his able management; but, as in former times, there was a Puthan faction which disliked the arrangement. Seetaram, like most of the higher class of Brahmins, understands Arabic, Persian, Sanscrit, and the Bengalee language; and his family had been for a great many years employed in the Bhopal principality. It has, at times, happened in that country, that some Puthan noblemen have been displeased at a Hindoo possessing the influence and powers of Deewan: but, the only remedy for such a state of things is, for the Puthan nobles to qualify themselves for office.

1835. This year the marriage of Secunder Bebee with the Nuwab Jehangier Mahomed Khan, was solemnized on the 18th of April, 1835.

1836. In 1836, the Guide and Gazetteer states that "Secunder Begum showed that she, also, had begun to be actuated by ambitious views, the discharge of the duties of the office of Ruler, and deeming it necessary to qualify herself for that she should see the country and the Purgunnah officers, she started on the tour of the districts" (161) The young Begum was now about 20 years of age, and it was not surprising that, at such an age, she should wish to learn to govern, and to desire to see her country, and judge for herself, from personal observation. She knew perfectly well that *Begum Sumroo* transacted her own public affairs, and gave her own directions in matters which she could not personally superintend, such as the command of her troops. (162) She knew the exact rent of each village of her Jaghier, and had some very fairly disciplined troops. The young Begum knew, by experience, that by the lamented death of her father (Nuwab Nuzzur Mahomed Khan) her mother had become Regent at an early age, and after a time took upon herself the conduct of public affairs, which she executed with much ability. The young Begum herself might, also, be placed in the same unfortunate position. The question of the *Purdah* (163) is one of

(161) Must mean Purgunnahs, so called in that country

(162) Mr Dyce Sombre, now so well known in Europe, had the general management of her affairs, under her general direction.

(163) *Purdah*. It must be, here, stated that when a Begum or princess transacts business in public, i. e. in the *Udalut*, or Court of Justice, she is not seen; but sits behind a lattice-worked

long established custom among Mahomedans. But it is a custom which does not prevent the female sovereign of a country from exercising in public the duties of the state. Without a proper knowledge gained by travelling through the country, and listening to complaints, how can a prince or princess select proper ministers, (164) or do justice to the people?

1837. It was at length settled, after a negotiation of some days, that the Nuwab,—having been previously placed on the musnud, or throne, on the 29th of November, 1837, the Begum mother assisting, and taking part in the ceremony,—should be inducted into the despatch of public business. In July, in the year 1838, Secunder Begum was delivered of a daughter

door, and hears what is said, and gives answers, and decides cases in person.

(164) The time has arrived when attention in India is being directed to the education of females, natives of India Nothing will more improve the minds and morals of the people, because it will raise the character of the women; and in all countries where the females are well educated, it is held to be a reproach to the men to be inferiorly educated. Good education tends much to social order, and respect to Governments. The ignorant cannot appreciate the measures of their superiors, so long as they are uneducated The well-educated *can* and will act as a check upon the licentious and disorderly. It is to be hoped that the *Vernacular* plan will be carried out. Until a useful education shall be given to the natives, by which they shall be enabled to understand the best mode of labouring in their calling, and to become acquainted with the more perfect systems of other nations; there will be no improvement in agriculture, or in the arts. European modes, modified, may be adopted with advantage to India.

1840. " In the year 1840, the political agent at Sehore (165) submitted a proposal for the reformation of the Bhopal contingent, which was approved of by the Governor General. The late Brigadier Anquetil, (166), was consulted as to the re-organization of the corps The Nuwab agreed to increase the tribute (167) paid for its maintenance from 130,000 to 138,000 rupees, in order to forward the completion of the projected reforms. The Cavalry were reduced from 300 to 256 sabres, and the Infantry from 653 to 528 fighting men, making a total of 784 men (168) The Infantry were thenceforth to have muskets instead of matchlocks, and an increased rate of pay. There were two guns attached to the corps. The corps to be commanded by a European commandant assisted by an Adjutant." (169)

It has been stated by Sir John *Malcolm*, (170) alluding to the exercise of authority by the Minister, that " The history of Bhopal, while this system continued, consists in the proceed-

(165) The late Mr Wilkinson, of the Madras Civil Service

(166) Killed in the retreat from Cabool in January, 1842.

(167) Or rather the contingent was kept up (must be understood) in lieu of paying tribute, though the 125,000 rupees proposed as tribute was given up in 1818

(168) The original numbers were Cavalry 600 and infantry 400, or total 1,000 men. The reform made the 784 men, with muskets, a more efficient corps than before; particularly with the addition of the guns.

(169) Gazetteer.

(170) Page 365

ings of the Dewans, or Ministers." (171) It will have been observed that since the death of Dost Mahomed Khan, the Founder, in 1723, most of the Deewans have managed the state affairs: except in the time of Vizier Mahomed Khan, and of Nuzzur Mahomed Khan—equal in military character to Dost Mahomed Khan; and the above named Nuwabs were even more accomplished than the Founder of the principality. It has been stated that the widow of Yar Mahomed Khan, greatly influenced the Councils of Bhopal for more than half a century. The Begum mother, when Regent of Bhopal, proved herself in every way, from her knowledge and acquirements, to be perfectly mistress of the art of Government: and her daughter, the present Begum of Bhopal, possesses high qualities for the exercise of the sovereign power; which has for some years been in her hands. These two princesses have

(171) They have chiefly been Hindoos. The reason of it is this, Hindoos, Brahmins in particular, have more application than Mahomedans. Scarcely any Hindoo of good family is to be found who is not able to read and write Persian, if not Arabic, with fluency and facility. A high caste Brahmin will generally possess a knowledge of the Sanscrit language Mahomedan noblemen and gentlemen read for their own amusement, and if possessed of property, do not like the drudgery of office Mooieed Mahomed Khan, proved a very bad Deewan. Jowlad Khan and Chutta Khan, were originally Hindoos When Vizier Mahomed Khan was Dewan, the country prospered His conduct of affairs proved his aptitude for the Nuwabship. At Hyderabad, *Chundoo Lal* (of the writer caste) has for a great many years been Deewan, or Minister at that Court.

never allowed the Minister to decide alone, on state questions, or on matters of consequence. It is to be hoped that measures may be adopted to improve the Bhopal principality, to the utmost of its means: and in accordance with the sincere desire of the ruling authorities ; for to use the words of Sir John *Malcolm*—"*Bhopal is at this moment, and will continue while well managed, an essential point of strength in Central India.*" (172)

(172) From an extract of a letter of the 13th December 1844, from Indore, it appears that the Nuwab of Bhopal, Jehanghir Mahomed Khan, died on the 9th of December, 1844. It is said that the daughter of the Nuwab, and of the present (Secunder) Begum of Bhopal will be the successor.

ERRATA.

Page 3, note 5, *for* "40" *read* "140 years."
—— 4,
—— 5,
—— 6,
—— 8, } *for* "puthan" *read* "Puthan."
—— 9,
—— 10,
—— 13,
—— 9, note 12, line 4, *for* "toh" *read* "to."
—— 17, *for* "Jowlad," *read* "Fowlad."
line 13, *for* "resolute," *read* "violent."
—— 19, line 4, *for* "Sahore," *read* "Sehore"
—— 38, line 14, *for* "an" *read* "no."
—— 43, line 14, *for* "Hylut," *read* "Hybut."
—— 46, line 5, *for* "he," *read* "be."
—— 52, note 62, *for* "Nowlut Rae Lal," *read* "Nowbut Lal"
—— 70, line 2, *after* "town," *put* ";".
—— 89, line 14, *for* "Soneepoor," *read* "Sonepoor."
—— 91, line 18, *for* "Sapgur," *read* "Saugor."
—— 107, line 5 in note, *after* "these," *put* a comma, and *after* "letters," *omit* comma.
—— 108, line 2, in note 131, *for* "Itchamur," *read* "Itchawur."
—— 112, note 138, *for* "Namdur" *read* "Namdar."
—— 115, note 142, line 9, before Baitool, *for* "or," *read* "and," *after* "Baitool," *add* "wanting."
—— 129, *read* line the second *before* the first line.
—— 132, line 9, in note 171, *for* "Jowlad," *read* "Fowlad."

Published by

Facsimile Publisher
Ashok Vihar, Delhi-110052 (India)
Website: www.facsimilepublishers.com

Distributed by

Gyan Books Pvt. Ltd.
5, Ansari Road, Daryaganj, New Delhi-110002 (India)
E-mail: books@gyanbooks.com, Website: www.gyanbooks.com

9 789333 198639